# Procedural Content Generation for Unity Game Development

Harness the power of procedural content generation to design unique games with Unity

**Ryan Watkins**

BIRMINGHAM - MUMBAI

# Procedural Content Generation for Unity Game Development

First published: January 2016

Production reference: 1220116

Published by Packt Publishing Ltd.
Livery Place
35 Livery Street
Birmingham B3 2PB, UK.

ISBN 978-1-78528-747-3

www.packtpub.com

# Credits

**Author**
Ryan Watkins

**Reviewers**
Joshua Byrom
Michele Pirovano
Till Riemer
Gennaro Vessio

**Acquisition Editor**
Prachi Bisht

**Content Development Editor**
Merint Thomas Mathew

**Technical Editor**
Vivek Arora

**Copy Editor**
Merilyn Pereira

**Project Coordinator**
Francina Pinto

**Proofreader**
Safis Editing

**Indexer**
Rekha Nair

**Graphics**
Jason Monteiro

**Production Coordinator**
Manu Joseph

**Cover Work**
Manu Joseph

# Disclaimer

# About the Author

**Ryan Watkins** was digitized and absorbed into his computer at an early age. In the digital realm, he learned the importance of video games and the balance they brought to the ecosystem of computing. Video games strive to always push the boundaries of what we know to be true while being a super-charged source of fun. Ryan formed friendships with many of the video games he encountered on his digital journeys, and in return, they shared the secrets of their creation with him. He has since returned to the physical world to share those secrets with the rest of us.

# About the Reviewers

**Joshua Byrom** has been programming and gaming for over two decades, and has written numerous articles on the subjects of game programming and artificial intelligence. Around the age of eight, he was introduced to computers by his father, which generated in him a deep interest for computer science, particularly computer programming.

Since then, Joshua has written code for companies such as BMC Solutions Inc., AutoTrader.com, and Elite Property Services LLC. He has also worked for the army, where he wrote genetic algorithms for the U.S. Military. Currently, he works as a software architect, where he develops and maintains web applications for local lawyers, realtors, and retailers.

In addition, Joshua writes programming articles for online publishing, runs a small business that creates and publishes independent mobile and web applications, and provides code consulting for indie start-ups.

Currently, Joshua is located in Newnan, GA, and when he isn't lost thousands of lines deep in code, he likes to read both prose and poetry, or play video games.

**Michele Pirovano** is a freelance game developer and game researcher based in Bergamo, Italy. He holds a PhD in computer science from the Politecnico di Milano, where he graduated with a thesis on the design of autonomous exergaming systems.

His main interest is the application of artificial intelligence, procedural content generation, and complex mathematical systems to video games. He has written many articles on the use of computational intelligence in games, and continues to investigate both serious games and applied AI.

He is also the founder of the independent one-man game development studio Curiosity Killed the Cat. He is currently working on *.Age*, a rogue-lite village simulation game. He also loves cats.

**Till Riemer** is a game developer from Germany. He is currently living in Copenhagen, where he is working on the upcoming RPG Expeditions: Viking at indie developer Logic Artists.

As a teenager, Till started to get into programming and has always been fascinated with the prospects of adaptive AI in video games. He joined the games industry as a programmer on the acclaimed RPG Blackguards at Daedalic in 2013, and recently received an MSc in games technology from the IT University of Copenhagen, where he conducted his master's thesis about the creation of procedural side quests for role-playing games. Previously, he received a BSc in computer science.

In his free time, he works on a side project called Drakk Navis, a ship-racing game for tablets, but also loves to sit down with a guitar once in a while. He is also part of the team organizing events for the Copenhagen Indie scene and has represented the Danish Global Game Jam organizers at GDC in 2015. You can follow him on Twitter at `@TillRiemer`.

**Gennaro Vessio** received the Laurea Magistrale degree in informatics from the Department of Informatics at the University of Bari, Italy. Currently, he is a PhD student of the same department. His research is currently focused on the application of formal methods to the design and analysis of routing protocols for mobile ad hoc networks.

Concerning procedural content generation, he investigated, together with other colleagues, a grammar-based approach to the procedural generation of the environment of an endless game.

# www.PacktPub.com

## Support files, eBooks, discount offers, and more

For support files and downloads related to your book, please visit www.PacktPub.com.

Did you know that Packt offers eBook versions of every book published, with PDF and ePub files available? You can upgrade to the eBook version at www.PacktPub.com and as a print book customer, you are entitled to a discount on the eBook copy. Get in touch with us at service@packtpub.com for more details.

At www.PacktPub.com, you can also read a collection of free technical articles, sign up for a range of free newsletters and receive exclusive discounts and offers on Packt books and eBooks.

https://www2.packtpub.com/books/subscription/packtlib

Do you need instant solutions to your IT questions? PacktLib is Packt's online digital book library. Here, you can search, access, and read Packt's entire library of books.

## Why subscribe?

- Fully searchable across every book published by Packt
- Copy and paste, print, and bookmark content
- On demand and accessible via a web browser

## Free access for Packt account holders

If you have an account with Packt at www.PacktPub.com, you can use this to access PacktLib today and view 9 entirely free books. Simply use your login credentials for immediate access.

*For my two favorite girls, Keira and Aela Rose.*

# Table of Contents

# Preface

This book is an introduction to Procedural Content Generation (PCG) and how it can be applied in the popular game engine, Unity3D. PCG is a powerful programming practice that is trending in modern video games. Though PCG is not a new practice, it has become even more powerful as technology has advanced and it looks to be a prominent component of future video games.

Throughout the course of this book, we will be learning the basis of procedural content generation, including theory and practice. You will start by learning what PCG is and what its uses are. You will then move into learning about pseudo random numbers and how they work with PCG to create unique gameplay.

After your introduction to PCG, you will dive in and build the core functionality of a 2D *Roguelike* game. This game will be heavily based on PCG practices so that you can experience what it takes to design and implement PCG algorithms. You will experience level generation, item generation, adaptive difficulty, music generation, and more. Lastly, we will move into 3D object generation by generating a 3D planet.

The aim of this book is to teach you about the theory of PCG while providing some simplified practical examples. By the end of the book, you should have a fundamental understanding of PCG and how it can be applied using Unity3D. This will all facilitate your further learning, research, and practice of PCG methods in video game development.

# What this book covers

*Chapter 1, Pseudo Random Numbers,* teaches you about the theory of procedural content generation (PCG). We will cover what PCG is and how it is used in video games. You will then learn about a useful component of randomization called Pseudo Random Numbers (PRN). We will cover what PRNs are, how they are used, and how they can help us implement PCG algorithms.

*Chapter 2, Roguelike Games,* teaches you about a prime example of procedural content generation, *Roguelike* games. We will cover some history of the origin of PCG and *Roguelike* games. We will then set up the Unity project foundation of our very own *Roguelike* game.

*Chapter 3, Generating an Endless World,* begins the implementation of your 2D *Roguelike* game. We will be creating a level that generates itself at runtime while the player explores. We will cover PCG algorithm design and useful data substructures. Then, we will put it together to implement the game world.

*Chapter 4, Generating Random Dungeons,* implements the sublevels of our Roguelike game. We will cover a different approach to level generation as we generate a full level layout at runtime. You will learn about some common approaches to this technique and implement one for yourself.

*Chapter 5, Randomized Items,* teaches you about randomly generating items. The items you generate will have differing properties so we will use some techniques to communicate this to the player. We will cover item spawning, interaction, and inventory storage.

*Chapter 6, Generating Modular Weapons,* teaches you about and how to implement a random modular weapon system. You will build upon what you learned in the previous chapter to add more complexity to item generation. These items will comprise a small set of pieces that are assembled at runtime.

*Chapter 7, Adaptive Difficulty,* crosses over into the field of Artificial Intelligence (AI) and teaches you about how AI and PCG are similar and related. You will learn about the PCG idea of adaptive difficulty, which is one part AI and one part PCG. You will then implement an adaptive difficulty system for your *Roguelike* game.

*Chapter 8, Generating Music,* shows you how PCG can even contribute to the music and sound content of a game. You will learn a little music theory; just enough to design a PCG algorithm for music generation. Then, you will implement a music generator for your Roguelike game that can generate music at runtime.

*Chapter 9, Generating a 3D Planet*, switches gears from 2D-based PCG to 3D-based PCG. We will have finished our core 2D Roguelike functionality and be working on a new project. This chapter will introduce the fundamentals of 3D object generation. You will then implement a 3D planet generator. Plus, as a bonus, you will implement a first person controller to take a closer look at your generated world.

*Chapter 10, Generating the Future*, discusses the most common methods of PCG used today and some ways to further your learning in the subject. We will also summarize some of the key points of what you learned throughout the book and how they relate to these PCG methods. We will lastly take a look at some ways that we can improve these PCG methods for the future.

# What you need for this book

This book uses the popular game engine Unity3D for all of its programming example implementations. At the time this book was written, Unity 5 was the current software version and all the code examples were written with Unity version 5.2.2. All of the code examples are written in the C# language.

You will need to download and install Unity3D onto your computer to follow the examples in this book. All that is required for this is Unity, as it will compile and run your code. It also comes with a code editor, MonoDevelop, which can be used to write your code. If you choose to use a different code editor, you may do so as well.

# Who this book is for

This book was written with Unity development beginners in mind, but it is best suited for intermediate Unity developers. You will get the most out of this book if you are familiar with Unity development and the C# language. However, there is plenty of theory and programming method information that a beginning user can benefit from as well. Throughout the book, there are reference links and information tips that will guide an inexperienced user to additional information that will help facilitate their learning.

# Conventions

In this book, you will find a number of styles of text that distinguish between different kinds of information. Here are some examples of these styles, and an explanation of their meaning.

Code words in text, database table names, folder names, filenames, file extensions, pathnames, dummy URLs, user input, and Twitter handles are shown as follows: "We can include other contexts through the use of the `include` directive."

A block of code is set as follows:

```
1 int integerVariable = 42;
2
3 int interger function (int inInteger) {
4    return inInteger + 42;
5 }
```

When we wish to draw your attention to a particular part of a code block, the relevant lines or items are set in bold:

```
1 int integerVariable = 42;
2
3 int interger function (int inInteger) {
4    return inInteger + 42;
5 }
```

**New terms** and **important words** are shown in bold. Words that you see on the screen, in menus or dialog boxes for example, appear in the text like this: "Click on the **Add component** button and add **Box 2D Collider** and **Sprite Renderer** components".

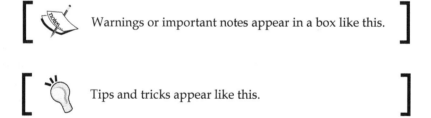

Warnings or important notes appear in a box like this.

Tips and tricks appear like this.

# Reader feedback

Feedback from our readers is always welcome. Let us know what you think about this book—what you liked or may have disliked. Reader feedback is important for us to develop titles that you really get the most out of.

To send us general feedback, simply send an e-mail to feedback@packtpub.com, and mention the book title via the subject of your message.

If there is a topic that you have expertise in and you are interested in either writing or contributing to a book, see our author guide on www.packtpub.com/authors.

# Customer support

Now that you are the proud owner of a Packt book, we have a number of things to help you to get the most from your purchase.

# Downloading the example code

You can download the example code files for all Packt books you have purchased from your account at http://www.packtpub.com. If you purchased this book elsewhere, you can visit http://www.packtpub.com/support and register to have the files e-mailed directly to you.

# Downloading the color images of this book

We also provide you with a PDF file that has color images of the screenshots/ diagrams used in this book. The color images will help you better understand the changes in the output. You can download this file from https://www.packtpub. com/sites/default/files/downloads/B04808_ColoredImages.pdf.

# Errata

Although we have taken every care to ensure the accuracy of our content, mistakes do happen. If you find a mistake in one of our books—maybe a mistake in the text or the code—we would be grateful if you would report this to us. By doing so, you can save other readers from frustration and help us improve subsequent versions of this book. If you find any errata, please report them by visiting http://www.packtpub.com/ submit-errata, selecting your book, clicking on the **Errata Submission Form** link, and entering the details of your errata. Once your errata are verified, your submission will be accepted and the errata will be uploaded on our website, or added to any list of existing errata, under the Errata section of that title. Any existing errata can be viewed by selecting your title from http://www.packtpub.com/support.

# Piracy

Piracy of copyright material on the Internet is an ongoing problem across all media. At Packt, we take the protection of our copyright and licenses very seriously. If you come across any illegal copies of our works, in any form, on the Internet, please provide us with the location address or website name immediately so that we can pursue a remedy.

Please contact us at copyright@packtpub.com with a link to the suspected pirated material.

We appreciate your help in protecting our authors, and our ability to bring you valuable content.

# Questions

You can contact us at questions@packtpub.com if you are having a problem with any aspect of the book, and we will do our best to address it

# 1
# Pseudo Random Numbers

This chapter will introduce the idea of procedural content generation and one highly useful component, pseudo random numbers. Later in the chapter, you will use pseudo random numbers to create a derivation of the classic `Hello World` program. For convenience, **procedural content generation** will be abbreviated to **PCG** for the remainder of the text. Let's also abbreviate **pseudo random numbers** to **PRNs**.

Here's a quick overview of what the chapter will cover and what you will learn:

- Define PCG: What it is and what you can do with it
- Discover PRN generation
- Learn how PRNs relate to PCG
- Use PRNs in our first program
- Develop a new randomized PCG like the `Hello World` program

In this chapter, we will complete a very simple step-by-step example. The example in this chapter will be simple enough to help introduce newcomers to Unity and also serve as a refresher to those coming back after some time away. However, it is important to remember that the successive examples will be much more involved. It is best that you are fundamentally familiar with Unity and C# scripting in Unity.

Unity Technologies offers a range of tutorials for beginners at `https://unity3d.com/learn/tutorials`.

You can also reference the Unity Documentation if you need to know the usage of any specific part of Unity at `http://docs.unity3d.com/Manual/index.html`.

Now, let's dive in and start learning.

# Introducing PCG

We begin our learning adventure with the broad concept of PCG. The key word here is **procedural**. A **procedure** in programming, simply put, is an instruction to be executed. Procedures are the main paradigm in computer programming. A script you write in Unity is just a set of instructions or procedures we want Unity to perform.

You use procedures, methods, or functions as a means to communicate the instructions you want the computer to complete. We can use these same procedures to instruct the computer to generate content in many different ways. We can apply this idea to a broad range of programming disciplines such as data visualization, dynamic advertising, and so on, but in this book, we are using it for video games.

If **procedural** is the *how* then **content** is the *what*. Content can be anything we are presenting to the user. In our `Hello World` example later in the chapter, our content will simply be text. However, video games have a wide range of assets that make up the content we want to deliver to a player.

Typically, we think of the levels, character models, and other art assets when we think of content in video games. But there is also textures, music, sounds, story, artificial intelligence, and more that together make up the content of a game. PCG is the concept or paradigm by which all these pieces of content can be generated with some well-written code. PCG can be applied to nearly all aspects of a game through scripting, and you will learn some of the main ways to do this throughout the book.

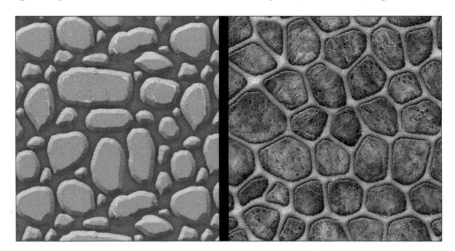

On the left is a hand-drawn texture, and on the right is a Procedurally Generated texture

What's exciting about PCG is that we can let the computer take some of the responsibilities of the designer by giving it some instructions and letting it create parts of the game world on its own. We might even be surprised by the results. As developers, we usually do not like being surprised by our script's actions, but in this case, it's part of the plan.

PCG can also come in a few different forms for practical use. We can generate content from scratch, such as the texture see earlier, or we can generate assets from a set of premade parts, such as generating a tavern scene from premade props such as tables, chairs, barrels, and crates. Another option, though, is providing tools to the player to take on the role of creating content. The player creating content isn't necessarily PCG but you will have created a PCG system that now takes user input as a parameter. A great example of this is the popular game *Minecraft* developed by Mojang.

A player-created building in the popular game *Minecraft*

*Minecraft* is also an example of one of the most popular uses of PCG, randomization. Players in Minecraft can make structures and break down the land around them. However, the game's entire landscape is based on randomization. Randomization is used in many games, both virtual and table top. Randomness introduces a chance factor that creates fun out of unpredictability.

However, the most important thing about randomness in video games is that it is almost impossible to achieve true randomness on a computer system. This is why we refer to them as pseudo random numbers, because they are technically not random. We will explore this aspect of randomness, or pseudo randomness, later in the chapter with PRNs.

# Usage of PCG

The reasons we might consider using PCG include unique, robustness, adaptability, and size. We might strive for our player to experience the game in their own truly unique play-through. We could use PCG to take the content that we have designed and make truly robust games that would take many hours to explore every inch of. We can make our game adapt to the player in interesting ways such as scaling the difficulty to easier or harder based on the actions of the player.

Size, though, is an interesting benefit to PCG. Well before games played with amazing HD graphics at 60 frames a second, they were mostly text based. Early computer systems were very limited both in processing power and storage memory. One of the earliest occurrences of PCG was in games that procedurally generated levels using ASCII characters. We can see an example of this in the game *Rogue* developed in the 1980s. We discuss Rogue and the subsequent sub-genre of games *Roguelike* in later chapters.

PCG was thus a solution, of sorts, to the fact that early computers really had no means to present graphics to the player. Graphics comprise the bulk of a game in terms of size taking a lot of processing power and memory. The procedurally generated ASCII levels of *Rogue* were calculated instead of being loaded from the file. This meant early computer systems could use memory and processing power as needed instead of needing a lot of memory all at once when you start a predefined game level.

We can also consider size savings in terms of our team as well. A designer/artist typically will need to make every piece of game content by hand. As games get larger, it becomes more difficult to create enough unique content within one game. Games lose their reward factor and players become bored easily when they see continuous repetition of in-game content. We then need to produce more content, which means more designers, artists, and individual assets. PCG helps alleviate this need by taking on some of the burden of producing unique content.

PCG can thus be viewed as a tool for the designer. There is a very creative facet to the idea of PCG. We can design pieces or modules of a whole, like a level or item, and use PCG to put them together in unique and interesting ways. We could also make 3D models, but then, we would have to generate the textures for them. Otherwise, we could generate full levels from scratch and add in some designed props. There are plenty of possibilities to fit the situation or team's needs.

Some of Gearbox Software's *Borderlands* procedurally generated weapons, each generated from asset modules

You also have a unique opportunity to create games that can expand infinitely (or close to it). We will see this later in the book when we learn how PCG can be used to create a game level that never ends. Are you convinced that PCG is an amazing game development component?

# Application of PCG

Where we can apply PCG is an interesting question, as it can theoretically be applied to every aspect of a game. Here is a brief list of examples of where it has already been used:

- Level layout—Blizzard Entertainment's *Diablo* series
- Unique item creation—Gearbox Software's *Borderlands* series

- AI behavior — Hisanori Hiraoka, Daisuke Watanabe, and Kyohei Fujita's *dreeps*
- Texture generation — Farbrausch's *.kkrieger*
- Model Generation — Speed Tree (which can be used with Unity)
- Storyline — Bethesda's *The Elder Scrolls 5: Skyrim* Radiant Quests system
- Music — Ed Key and David Kanaga's *Proteus*

This list encapsulates some of the more popular uses of PCG. As a game lover, you are encouraged to research each of these games as they are wonderful examples of PCG. We will cover most of these topics in this book, but this is by no means an exhaustive list of how PCG can be used in game development.

So now you know what PCG is but what about implementing it? To put it plainly, PCG is just the idea that we can automatically generate game content. We will develop different algorithms and use certain programming practices to apply the idea of PCG to our video games.

One of the more popular ways to implement PCG utilizes randomness or random events to produce content. It is popular because it is easier to let randomness determine certain events over scripting every outcome. For example, we might let randomness determine which pieces are used to generate the weapons seen previously in Gearbox's *Borderlands*. We might use a pseudo random number generator and bind each piece of the weapon to a randomly determined number. Of course, keep in mind that this isn't truly random as we will soon discuss further.

# Pseudo random numbers

Random numbers have been used in games for a very long time, from traditional card games to dice rolling in table-top games. Random numbers add a chance factor to games that make them exciting and forever unpredictable. The unpredictability of a game is exciting because it always offers a unique experience. You can introduce this randomness factor into your games with a little computer science in the form of a PRN generator.

PRNs and PRN generators are a highly researched subject in computer science, as they are central to cryptography and cyber security. If you ever look into cryptography, you'll find it heavily steeped in complicated mathematics. Luckily, Unity has a very easy method to generate random numbers. Certainly, the complexity of secure number generation isn't required for video games. Nonetheless, it is important to understand some of the theories behind what seems like magic.

# Random versus pseudo random numbers

The most important distinction to make is that PRNs are not random numbers. A truly random event would be something like a die roll. We could write some sort of physics simulation to simulate a die roll to achieve a random number. We could also take the static from a TV screen and plot it on an XY plane and take a single point to represent a random number. However, PRNs are preferred in game programming because they are easier to generate. The preceding examples would take too much processing power as they are a fairly complex idea. But a PRN generator is an equation that calculates a string of numbers. This also produces an added benefit of being able to find our way back to a certain generated result.

You could generate a more random sequence of numbers by grabbing points off our TV static graph, but what if you want to reproduce a result? Imagine we created an entire planet using a specific sequence of random numbers. Unless we generate that planet the first time, record the sequence used, and ship the game with the sequence included in the code, we might never be able to reproduce those results again.

Now imagine we generated trillions of planets. We would have to somehow come up with a system to store all the results of generating each planet on the first run. That just sounds unwieldy. A PRN generator, however, uses a seed number to generate a sequence, which will eventually repeat. So, instead of saving all the information needed to generate the planets, we just need the PRN generator equation and seed to regenerate all the planets at runtime.

Random number noise signals – on the left is a random number pattern
that does not repeat and on the right is a PRN pattern that repeats

A **seed** in reference to PRNs, is simply a number either designated by you or by some other pseudo random means. The Unity Random method will acquire a seed from the system time if you don't provide one. The seed of a PRN generator can be stored as a variable like you would store any number in a script. This is useful when we need to recreate the sequence. We just plug our seed back into our number generator and get the same sequence again.

For example, imagine we used a sequence of PRNs to create a level. Let's say the numbers represent whether a room, a hallway, or a trap is placed in a certain area. Now, a player has just finished that level and we decide to delete the level to save space in the memory. But later, the player gets a quest that requires them to go back to that same level. If we keep the seed number we used to generate the level, we can put the seed back into our number generator, get the original sequence, and remake the level as it was initially.

As stated earlier, one of the side effects of PRN generation is that it is cyclical. There comes a point in which the PRN generator generates the seed again, starting the process over. This is important to consider as it might become a cause of repetition in some of your procedurally generated content. There are multiple factors in avoiding repetition, such as the size of the number, the value, and the sequence range. Unity's Random method should be enough for most cases though.

So, in short, you know that PRNs are not random numbers but they are close enough. The key points are:

- PRN generators need a seed value
- You should store the seed value so we can easily recreate the PRN sequence
- PRN generators will eventually repeat
- If repetition becomes a problem, look into creating a more complex equation for a longer seed range

PRNs are cool and all, but how are they used?

# PRNs in PCG

You can use PRNs as a decision driver to PCG. As a developer you want to be concerned about minimizing minor detail decisions. These decisions could be tasks such as placing every single tree by hand in a forest scene. You want the scene to look realistic but placing all of them yourself could be very time consuming. You can use PCG for some of this decision making. Using some directed randomness to build the forest for you saves a massive amount of time.

A forest scene created with Unity Terrain Engine which uses PRNs

So it's time to get our hands on this! As previously stated, PRN generation can be a complicated mathematical problem but Unity has a built-in class for us called `Random`. Now, let's get exposed to PRNs in our first PCG example.

## Random Hello World

We are going to start with an age-old classic programming example, the `Hello World` program. If you have been programming for a while, you likely have done one or more of these already. There will be a twist though. We are going to use PRNs to randomize how we say `Hello World`.

Be aware that this book is using Unity 5.2.2. Some of the examples will be incompatible with earlier versions.

# Classic Hello World

Let's begin by setting up the project and completing the classic Hello World program. Start by launching Unity and creating a new project. You can name it Hello World. You can also set the perspective to 2D since most of what we do in this book will be in 2D.

Unity launch screen

Once the project is loaded, we will create a new Text GameObject in order to render our Hello World to the screen. On the top toolbar, select **GameObject | UI | Text**. This will place a new Canvas object with a Text object child onto the scene. An EventSystem is also placed in the **Hierarchy** panel but you can ignore this.

If you are unfamiliar with or would like to know more about Unity's UI features, Unity Technologies offers video lessons on the topic. You can find them at http://unity3d.com/learn/tutorials/topics/user-interface-ui.

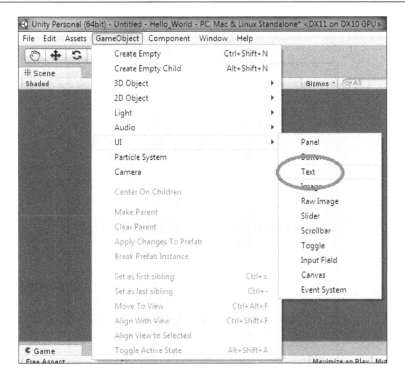

Canvas is mostly off screen and you have to zoom out quite a lot to see the full view. Rather than zooming out, let's adjust the Canvas to occupy the Main Camera view space, as follows:

1. Select **Canvas**.
2. Select the **Render Mode** dropdown in the **Canvas** component section.
3. Select **Screen Space - Camera**.
4. This will open up a new field called **Render Camera**.
5. From the **Hierarchy** pane, drag and drop the **Main Camera** object into the **Render Camera** field.

This will adjust your **Canvas** object to fit the **Main Camera** view. You might still need to zoom out slightly to see the edges of **Canvas**.

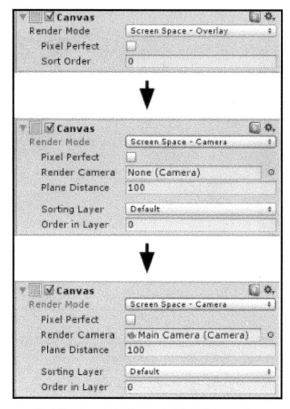

Workflow to get the Canvas in Main Camera view

You might have noticed at this point that there is some text on the screen. In the lower left corner of the **Canvas**, it says **New Text** in a default grey that is difficult to see. Let's change that.

Select the **Text** object, which is a child of the **Canvas** object. First, we will change the position. In the **Rect Transform** component section:

1. Select the value in the **Pos X** field and change it to 0.
2. Repeat for the **Pos Y** field.

The anchors are set to center so the **Rect** should snap to the center of the **Canvas**. Next, we'll change the size of the **Rect** so that we can make the text larger:

1. Select the **Width** field and change it to 500.
2. Select the **Height** field and change it to 65.

This will allow us to have much larger text. Note that if we had just tried to change the font size without changing the **Rect** size, the text would be clipped or would even vanish completely. Now let's get the text looking nice by going to the **Text (Script)** component section:

1.  Under **Character**, select the **Font Size** field and change it to 55.

2.  Under **Paragraph**, select the center alignment button.

3.  Select the **Color** field and change it to white.

 The center alignment button appears as  in the Unity Editor.

Now our text is nice and visible. At this point, you can select the text in the **Text** field and delete it. We are going to have our script write the text for us.

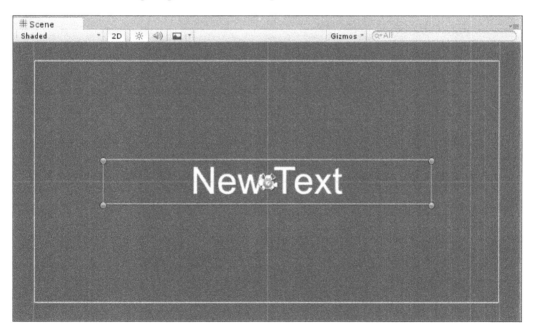

Finished canvas and text formatting

Let's start scripting by creating a new C# script. On the top toolbar, select **Assets | Create | C# Script**. This will create a new script in your **Assets** folder under the **Project** pane. You can name the script `HelloWorld.cs`.

Open the script in MonoDevelop or your favorite IDE. We are going to use the following *Code Snip 1.1*:

```
1 using UnityEngine;
2 using UnityEngine.UI;
3 using System.Collections;
4
5 public class HelloWorld : MonoBehaviour {
6
7   public Text textString;
8
9   void Start () {
10     textString.text = "Hello World";
11   }
12 }
```

**Downloading the example code**

You can download the example code files for all Packt books you have purchased from your account at http://www.packtpub.com. If you purchased this book elsewhere, you can visit http://www.packtpub.com/support and register to have the files e-mailed directly to you.

Let's take a look at what's happening in *Code Snip 1.1*:

- `Line 2`: Be sure to include `UnityEngine.UI` or you won't be able to access the `Text` component
- `Line 7`: This is our public `Text` object, which we will define in the Unity editor
- `Line 10`: At the start of the scene, we will take our text object and assign the string `Hello World` to it.

That's all there is to it. Now, we just need to add the script to the scene. It doesn't matter which object you attach the `HelloWorld.cs` script to because we will declare the specific `Text` object the script acts on. To keep things organized, this way works well:

1. Drag and drop the `HelloWorld.cs` script from the **Assets** folder to the **Text** object on the scene.
2. Drag and drop the **Text** object from the **Hierarchy** pane to the **Text String** field in the **Hello World (Script)** component of the **Text** object.

Now, you can press the play button, and you'll see **Hello World** in a large font:

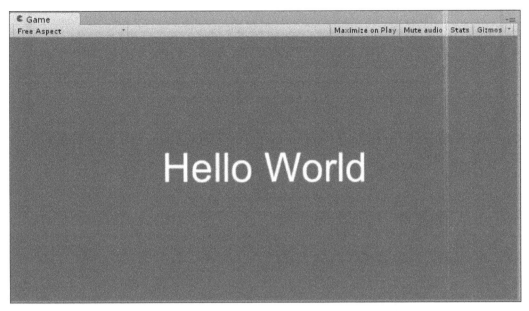

Hello World program's result

That completes the `Hello World` program. However, that's not all that interesting. In order to give this classic programming example some new flair, let's add some randomness.

## PCG Hello World

Using our `Hello World` example, we will add PRNs into the mix and give our program some procedurally generated text. We'll start by editing our current `HelloWorld.cs` script. The goal here is to randomly display one of a few variations of the Hello World text.

You can achieve this by creating an array of different strings and having Unity's Random method choose a number from 0 to the length of the array. You will use that PRN as the index of the string array. In this case, our array holds the Hello World string in a few different languages. So instead of telling the `Text` object to display **Hello World**, we will tell it to display the contents of the array at the PRN index.

Unity's Random.Range has a usage of (inclusive, exclusive). In our code, we use Random.Range (0, 4), which means 0 will be in the selected range but the range stops at 3. One reason for this is if we have a C# list, we can write the range as (0, List.Count) instead of (0, ListCount - 1).

You can find more information on Unity's Random at http://docs.unity3d.com/ScriptReference/Random.html.

Open the HelloWorld.cs script and make the following changes in *Code Snip 1.2*:

```
5 public class HelloWorld : MonoBehaviour {
6
7   public string[] hellos = new string[4] {
        "Hello World", "Hola Mundo",
        "Bonjour Le Monde", "Hallo Welt"};
8
9   public Text textString;
10
11  void Start () {
12    Random.seed = (int)System.DateTime.Now.Ticks;
13    int randomIndex = Random.Range (0, hellos.Length);
14    textString.text = hellos[randomIndex];
15  }
16 }
```

The changes in *Code Snip 1.2* are as follows:

- Line 7: Here you will declare a string array that we can call hellos, which will hold all our Hello World strings.

- Line 12: This is the PRN generator seed, which we discussed earlier in the chapter. We are picking a random number to seed the generator. The seed comes from your computer's current time in processor ticks (which is somewhere around a millisecond).

- Line 13: Here, we call Random.Range to choose a PRN from 0 to 3, which will be the index of hellos that we choose to display.

- Line 15: This line is a modification from our previous example; here, we set the text display to our randomly selected Hello World string.

Head back into the Unity editor to see the changes. You should see the new **Hellos** field. If you expand it, then you will see all of the strings contained in the array. The script might also lose connection to the **Text** object. You can just drag and drop the **Text** object into the **Text String** field to reconnect it.

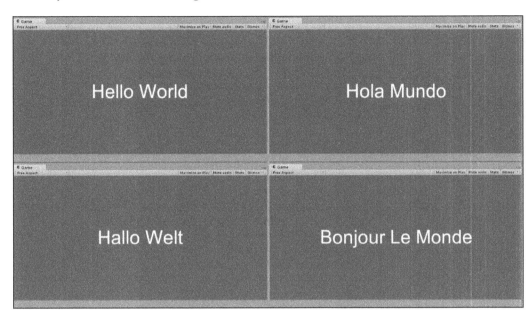

Hello World with PRNs program result

And that's it. You completed your first PCG capable program. Test it out by pressing the play button. You will randomly get one of the four `Hello World` strings displayed in the **Game** screen. There are only four choices so you might have to try a couple of times before you start seeing any variation.

# Challenge

As an added challenge, you can turn this into a die simulator. Try on your own to have the script display a random number from 1-6. You can, instead of displaying text, display an image of a die face. Also, see if you can display the image and store the random number corresponding to the die face for reference.

You can also try changing the seed to a number of your choice. If you play the scene with a constant number, you will get the same result every time. Try different numbers for different results. This is the benefit of the seed value; even though we are introducing a bit of randomness to our game, we have a way to control it. We will explore the seed value further in a later chapter.

# Summary

So you learned quite a bit of theory in this chapter and just touched the surface of how to apply it to games in Unity. You went over an introduction to PCG and why and how to use it. You were also introduced to PRNs and to how they are generated. We discussed what makes PRNs different from your average random number and the benefit a seed provides. You also learned why and how to use PRNs and then completed an example expanding on the classic `Hello World` program.

So what's left? Well, we are gearing up to build a fully functional game throughout this book. We are going to look at some of the more popular applications of PCG in video games. In the next chapter, we are going to briefly get acquainted with *Roguelike* games, which is a popular game subgenre. Roguelike games are known for their procedurally generated content, so it is a perfect fit for our learning adventure.

# 2
# Roguelike Games

This chapter will introduce a popular video game subgenre known for its use of PCG, called *Roguelike*. In the second half of the chapter, we will be setting up our *Roguelike* project, which will be used for the rest of the book. Here is an overview of what to expect in this chapter:

- Discovering *Roguelike* games
- Learning why *Roguelike* is a perfect fit for our PCG project
- Setting up our project

This chapter will begin our intermediate level work in Unity. From this point onward, it is best that you have a fundamental knowledge of the Unity Editor and C# scripting. As a reminder, this project was built using the current version of Unity (5.2.2), so there will be some incompatibilities with previous versions. The files used to set up the project will be included in the accompanying files under Chapter 2. However, all of the code files will be covered in the chapter for those of you who prefer to write them out yourselves.

We will be working from an existing project including both art and code assets. The art files that are included have some dependencies that need to be set. There is a Unity package included, which can be imported, that will contain all the prebuilt art dependencies. All of the art files will be explained that will aid your overall understanding of the project structure. If you are comfortable with 2D sprite animations, you are welcome to use your own art.

Now, let's discuss PCG in *Roguelike* games.

# An introduction to Roguelike games

Roguelike is a subgenre of the genre **Role-playing Game** (**RPG**). Its name originates from a game called *Rogue* released in 1980 by Michael Toy and Glenn Wichman. Rogue is known for its use of PCG, particularly in level creation. The game used a tile-based level generation system, in particular ASCII characters were used to represent tiles.

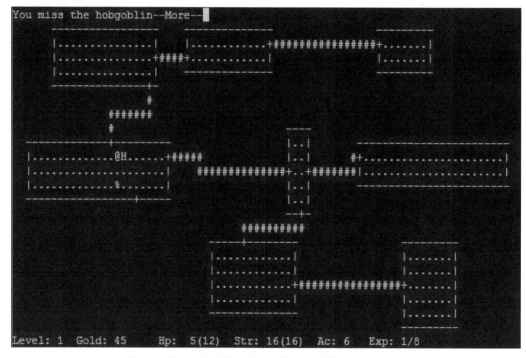

Image of *Rogue* (1980) by Michael Toy and Glenn Wichman

A tile is a small piece of art, typically depicting land or ground that can be laid out like a game board. Imagine a Chess or Checkers board, but each square can be replaced with a small rectangular picture. In tile-based games, it is typical that the player character only occupies a single tile space at a time. Our *Roguelike* game will use a tile-based level generator, as well.

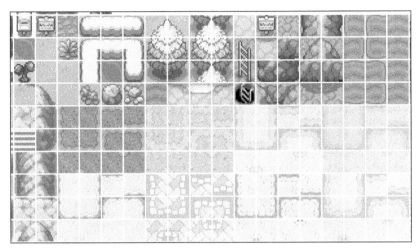

Tile sprite sheet from the popular game, *Pokemon*, developed by Game Freak

Other typical traits and gameplay mechanics of *Roguelike* games include 2D graphics, random player items, turn-based gameplay, and permanent player character death. Games that mimic the 1980's *Rogue* have been popular among the indie game market. *Roguelike* games' use of PCG makes them ideal for easier art asset production and potentially cheaper to develop.

# Why Roguelike?

The fact that *Roguelike* games are dependent on PCG makes them an ideal candidate to learn this topic. Also, working in 2D will simplify our algorithms so that we can focus on the theory of PCG. An added bonus is that *Roguelike* games are fairly popular, so there are some really helpful resources out there that can aid you in your learning. We will even use one such resource, which is a tutorial from Unity Technologies itself.

# Our own Roguelike project

So now that you know a little more about *Roguelike* games and why we are going to use them to learn about PCG, let's take a look at our main project. This project will use a predefined art asset group and code base. We will be getting these assets from the Unity Technologies tutorial *2D Roguelike*. This tutorial was actually the inspiration for this book, so it's only fitting that we showcase some of it.

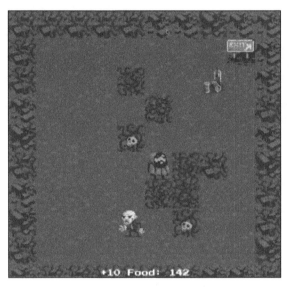

Unity Technologies' 2D Roguelike—courtesy of Unity Technologies

The full Unity 2D Roguelike tutorial can be found at `https://unity3d.com/learn/tutorials/projects/2d-roguelike-tutorial`.

All the assets used in the tutorial are available via the Unity Asset Store at `https://www.assetstore.unity3d.com/en/#!/content/29825`.

Even though we are using the assets from Unity's 2D *Roguelike*, this won't be a recreation of the tutorial. We want to explore more of what PCG has to offer, so we will only be using a portion of Unity's original tutorial. Also, having the art assets predefined in this way will be helpful in allowing us to dive right into the PCG development.

# Setting up the project

Let's set up our base project. There will be two methods we will cover in setting up this project. You can either import the provided Unity package or you can follow through the code explanations in the *File Overview* section and write the code by hand. Either way, it is highly advised that you read through the code explanations to understand the structure of how the project operates.

# Importing the base project

We will import a package that will contain more assets and use them right away. However, keep in mind that we will use all the assets eventually. All of the files are explained in the *File Overview* section of this chapter:

1.  Start by opening up Unity and creating a new project. Select **2D** and then **Create Project**. We won't need to import any Standard Asset packages for this project.

2.  Once in **Unity Editor**, navigate to **Assets | Import Packages | Custom Package...** from the top menu bar. Navigate to the directory where you saved the code files that accompany this book. In the Chapter 2 folder, select the Chapter2Assets.unitypackage and open it. You will get a pop-up displaying all the assets in the package. You can click on **OK** and Unity will import the package.

3.  After the package has been imported, there might be a warning message that you can disregard for now. You now have several more folders in your Assets folder. Navigate to the Scenes folder and open the **Main** scene.

4.  You will see some game objects in your **Hierarchy** panel and some text on the screen of your **Game** view panel. You can now click on the play button to see a small animated character. You can move the character using the *W, A, S,* and *D* keys or the arrow keys.

Take notice of the character's movement. The character moves the width of a tile and is on a turn-based timing system. When a key is hit, the player character will move in that direction and into the adjacent tile; they will then wait for the enemies to take a turn. There are no enemies, so the player can move the character again immediately.

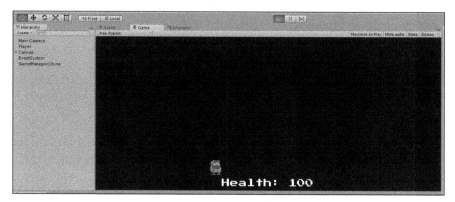

Results of importing the package and clicking on play

# File overview

Let's go over the files so that we understand how the project is structured. First, your folder structure should follow this format:

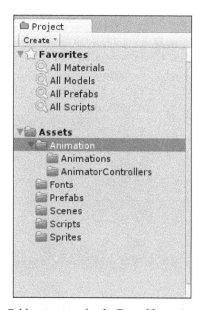

Folder structure for the Roguelike project

# Animation

In the `Animation` folder, there are two subfolders, `Animations` and `AnimatorControllers`. The `Animations` folder contains three sprite animations that the player character uses. The `AnimatorControllers` folder contains the animator controller that the player character uses to run its animations. These files are already integrated into the **Player** prefab from the `Chapter 2` import package.

# Fonts

The `Fonts` folder contains the font file `PressStart2P-Regular.ttf` and the Open Font License. You can disregard the license. The font is already applied to the text that is visible in our game preview.

# Prefabs

The `Prefabs` folder holds the tile set we will use to create our game board in the next chapter. This also holds `GameManager` and `Player`, which are being used to run our base project. **Player** is referenced directly on the **Hierarchy** panel and the `GameManager` is referenced via a script in the Main Camera.

- The **Player** prefab requires the **BoxCollider2D**, **RigidBody2D**, and **SpriteRenderer** components and the `Player.cs` script
- The **GameManager** prefab requires the `GameManager.cs` script
- `Wall` prefabs require a **BoxCollider2D** and **SpriteRenderer** component and the `Wall.cs` script
- The **OuterWall** prefabs require a **BoxCollider2D** and **SpriteRenderer** component
- The **Floor** prefabs requires a **SpriteRenderer** component

# Scenes

The `Scenes` folder holds our main scene. This is where our base game is set up and it is where we will add all our features. The **Hierarchy** panel shows what the scene holds.

The Main Camera is included in every Unity scene; this holds our **GameManager** prefab. The **Player** prefab holds the player character animations and functionality. The Canvas object contains a text object called **HealthText**, which is the source of the in-game text currently showing. The **EventSystem** object accompanies the **Canvas** object by default.

# Scripts

The `Scripts` folder contains all the scripts needed to run our base game. Some of the scripts are meant as hooks for future features. We will go over all the script files that came in the Unity package and discuss the relevant parts.

The first script is `BoardManager.cs,` as seen in *Code Snip 2.1:*

```
1 using UnityEngine;
2 using System;
3 using System.Collections.Generic;
4 using Random = UnityEngine.Random;
5
6 public class BoardManager : MonoBehaviour
7 {
  [Serializable]
8   public class Count
9   {
10     public int minimum;
11     public int maximum;
12
13     public Count (int min, int max)
14     {
15       minimum = min;
16       maximum = max;
17     }
18   }
19 }
```

The `BoardManager` script, so far, only holds a `Serializable` public class called `Count`, which we will use to aid us in randomizing our game board tiling. We can also use this class for any type of list randomization, such as placing items and enemies on the game board. The `BoardManager` script will be called by the `GameManager` script at the start of the game to set up the level.

Let's take a look at the code itself:

- Line 3: `System.Collections.Generic` allows us to use C# lists, which will come in handy later.
- Line 4: There are actually two random classes within Unity. One is the Unity class and the other is the .NET class. This line says that we want to use the Unity-specific `Random` method. The reason for this is the Unity `Random` method is optimized for game development.

- Line 8: The class, Count, is declared Serializable so that we can see the class's properties while in the Unity Editor.

- Lines 11-12: These are the properties Count will keep a track of. We will use minimum and maximum as a random range.

- Lines 14-18: This is the class constructor.

For more information on script serialization and the serializable key word, visit the Unity Documentation at http://docs.unity3d.com/ScriptReference/Serializable.html and http://docs.unity3d.com/Manual/script-Serialization.html.

The Loader.cs script is responsible for instantiating the GameManager class, which runs the essential parts of our game. You can see the script in the following *Code Snip 2.2*:

```
1 using UnityEngine;
2 using System.Collections;
3
4 public class Loader : MonoBehaviour
5 {
6   public GameObject gameManager;
7
8   void Awake ()
9   {
10    if (GameManager.instance == null)
11      Instantiate(gameManager);
12  }
13 }
```

Lines 8-12 are an important part of this script. The Awake function simply creates a new GameManager if one doesn't exist already. So let's discuss the GameManager.cs script, which is the connection point for all the other scripts.

The GameManager.cs script is too large to print in the middle of the chapter, so it can be found in the *Appendix* section under *Code Snip 2.3*. Instead, we will overview the functions that comprise the script.

- Awake(): The Awake function establishes the GameManager as a singleton, it sets up an enemy list (which we will use later), and initializes the game.

Singletons are programming paradigms in which only one singleton can exist during the program's runtime. This means that there is only ever one GameManager for every scene/level in our game.

For more information on singletons in Unity, visit http://wiki.unity3d.com/index.php/Singleton.

- OnLevelWasLoaded (int index): This function will track our dungeons when we create them.

- InitGame(): InitGame only clears the enemy list, which will be more useful when we actually have enemies. This will be the function we call to initialize our main level.

- Update(): The Update function checks whether it is the player's turn or the enemy's turn. Since there are no enemies yet, it is always the player's turn.

- GameOver(): When called, this function will disable the GameManager class.

- MoveEnemies(): This is called when it is the enemy's turn to move. There are currently no enemies, so this function just creates a pause letting the player character complete its move before another one can be taken. Having this structure predefined will make it easier to add in enemies later.

Next, we will take a look at the Wall.cs script, which gives properties to certain tiles that can block the player's movement. You see the Wall.cs script in *Code Snip 2.4*:

```
1 using UnityEngine;
2 using System.Collections;
3
4 public class Wall : MonoBehaviour
5 {
6   public Sprite dmgSprite;
7   public int hp = 3;
8
9   private SpriteRenderer spriteRenderer;
10
11  void Awake ()
12  {
13    spriteRenderer = GetComponent<SpriteRenderer> ();
14  }
15
16  public void DamageWall (int loss)
17  {
18    spriteRenderer.sprite = dmgSprite;
```

```
19
20    hp -= loss;
21
22    if(hp <= 0)
23       gameObject.SetActive (false);
24  }
25 }
```

This script won't be visibly useful until we write the code that will lay out our game board. For now, the script dictates that if there is a wall, it will block the player and some walls are destructible. Let's go through *Code Snip 2.4*:

- `Line 6`: We will store a reference to the sprite that will show a wall has taken damage.

- `Line 7`: Here, we will store the number of times a wall is hit before it is destroyed.

- `Lines 9-14`: The `Awake` function will store a reference to the **SpriteRenderer** component of our **Wall** prefab.

- `Lines 16-24`: The `DamageWall` function will track the times a wall is hit, switch out sprites to show wall damage, and eventually destroy a wall that has been hit enough.

The last few scripts are related in a sense. The `MovingObject.cs` script is an abstract class, meaning it can't be applied directly to our game. Instead, the `Player.cs` and `Enemy.cs` script inherit from the `MovingObject` class. The reason for this is the **Player** and **Enemy** prefabs will move in a similar way, so instead of writing the movement logic twice, we write it once and have both prefabs use it.

Because the `MovingObject.cs` script holds most of the movement logic, it is a larger file. So instead of printing it here, you can view it in the *Appendix* under *Code Snip 2.5*. As an alternative, we will overview the code as we did with the `GameManager.cs` script:

- `Start()`: The `Start` function stores the `BoxCollider2D` and `RigidBody2D` components attached to the Wall prefab. It also stores the reciprocal of a variable called `moveTime`, which is used to time the character's movement. We store the reciprocal here so that we can multiply the move time instead of dividing it later. Multiplication is computationally more efficient than division in most cases.

- `Move(int xDir, int yDir, out RaycastHit2D hit)`: `Move` checks whether the player can move in the direction they have input. The function casts a ray out from the player character in the direction input and if it hits anything, it returns `false`. The `RaycastHit2D` parameter hit, has a key word out so that it can be modified in the function and the effect is carried to outside the scope of the function.

- `SmoothMovement (Vector3 end)`: This is a coroutine for moving units from one tile space to the next. It takes a `Vector3` parameter, end, to specify where to the movement destination.

 For more information on coroutines, visit `http://docs.unity3d.com/Manual/Coroutines.html`.

- `AttemptMove<T>(int xDir, int yDir)`: `AttemptMove` is called by `Move` to check whether the player/enemy is being blocked from moving. It takes a generic parameter `T` to specify the type of component we expect our unit to interact with if blocked. This makes the function usable for any case of blocking action. Walls block a player's movement, but so will enemies. The virtual keyword means `AttemptMove` can be overridden by inheriting classes using the override keyword.

- `OnCantMove<T>(T component)`: `OnCantMove` will be called when a player/ enemy character is blocked from moving. There will be some logic here on how to handle certain blocking events. This function is abstract, which means it has no meaning in `MovingObjects`. However, any child classes will have a unique implementation of this function.

Now that we've seen the base class for our characters, let's take a look at the most important character class, the `Player` class. This script is another one that is too large to print here, so you can find it in the *Appendix* section under *Code Snip 2.6*. Here is an overview of the `Player.cs` script:

- First off, this class inherits from the `MovingObject` class, not `MonoBehaviour`.

- `Start()`: Here, we store the animator, get a reference to health points, set up the health point text, and call the `MovingObeject` base `Start` function.

- `Update()`: The `Update` function listens for player input and calls for movement.

- `AttemptMove<T>(int xDir, int  yDir)`: This is an override function whose base is in the `MovingObject` class. For now, it just calls the base `AttemptMove` function and updates the player's turn. Later, we will add into this function.

- `OnCantMove<T>(T component)`: This is another override function. We check whether we hit a wall here. If we hit a destructible wall, we will attack it.

- `LoseHealth(int loss)`: Here, we will manage our player character losing health when we add enemies.

- `CheckIfGameOver()`: Finally, this is just a check for ending the game when our player runs out of health. Again, this is going to be relevant when we add enemies.

Last is our `Enemy` script. Like the `Player` class, this also inherits from the `MovingObject` class. It can be viewed in *Code Snip 2.7*:

```
1  using UnityEngine;
2  using System.Collections;
3
4  public class Enemy : MovingObject
5  {
6    protected override bool AttemptMove <T> (int xDir, int yDir)
7    {
8       return true;
9    }
10
11   protected override void OnCantMove <T> (T component)
12   {
13   }
14 }
```

This class holds no logic at the moment. It has the two override functions that are required for the class to exist, but they are empty. We are using this script currently to add a delay in the player's movement. We are implementing a turn-based system so we check for enemy movement and because there is none, it's the player's turn again. Having this script predefined will save us some time later. However, since the script inherits from the `MoveingObject` class, the system requires the placeholder override function at a minimum.

So that's all there is to the base project. You can use your own art assets if you like. In fact, at the very least, you should try replacing the current art assets with your own at some point during your reading. This is good practice for learning Unity in general. Just be sure they meet the setup requirements, as explained in the *Prefabs* section.

# Summary

We just finished setting up our base project. Doing this will allow us to focus less on developing common gaming mechanics and more on PCG development. We also took a look at *Roguelike* games and how they uses PCG in tile based level generation.

During this chapter, you learned about the RPG subgenre *Roguelike*, which is an ode to the 1980's game, *Rogue*. We talked about the *Roguelike* game's inherent use of PCG, which is the reason we are developing one. And we set up our base project from which we will be developing our game. Now, we are ready to start learning how to build some PCG logic.

In the next chapter, you will put what you've learned about `Random` numbers and *Roguelike* games to work. We will be using our floor and wall tiles to build an endless game world.

# 3
# Generating an Endless World

Our base project is setup and ready to be expanded upon. You received an intro to PRNs and PCG by making a quick `Hello World` program. However, it is time to develop a fully functional PCG algorithm that can be directly applied to our *Roguelike* game.

Our game has the base functionality of a player character capable of movement by player input. In this chapter, we will create the tile-based Game Board that the player will explore. This Game Board will expand itself as the player moves, and as there are no bounds, the board is potentially infinite. In this chapter, you can expect:

- To learn about dynamic data structures
- To design our first PCG algorithm
- To set up a scene that allows for an ever expanding game world
- To develop our PCG Game Board

By the end of the chapter, you will have developed a PCG game world that is unique with every play. Plus, you will have achieved this with a relatively small amount of assets. We have to do some learning and planning first. So let's get started on the endless PCG Game Board.

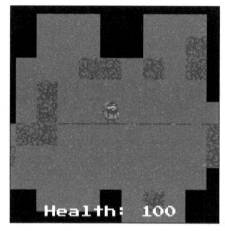

This is what our Roguelike endless PCG Game Board will look like

# Data structure choice

The first PCG algorithm we will develop will create the game environment that our player will explore. We are going to build a game world that never ends; that is, as long as you have enough memory. As the player explores the world, our algorithm will create and place more pieces of the Game Board.

Remember, the Game Board is what we are calling the ground area in which the player will walk on. The Game Board is made up of small, rectangular, 2D sprites that we refer to as **tiles**. In this chapter, we will start with floor tiles, which the player will walk on. We will then randomly add wall tiles to a new layer as an obstacle to the player.

The concept of the 2D Game Board can be visualized as a grid. A grid can be easily implemented as an array or list data structure to track the tiles we layout for the Game Board. As the player explores, we will add to our list references to our newly created tiles. We can then use this list to look up any tile on our Game Board. The most important role of the tile list is such that we don't recreate a tile that is already on the Game Board. This process is usually referred to as **object pooling**.

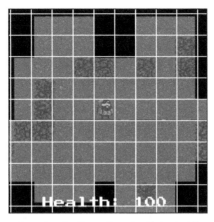

Imagine the Game Board within a grid

# Array

Because we are creating a large part of the Game Board while the player is playing the game, we need a data structure in which we can add tiles too dynamically. A two-dimensional array is visualized as a grid, which makes adding tile coordinates more natural. We name an index of a two-dimensional array like this: myArray[X] [Y]. X and Y will be the 2D $x$ axis and $y$ axis coordinates.

*Dynamic* is another computer science term. We refer to things as *static* or *dynamic*. Static refers to something that has a hard-coded value such as: const int num = 2;. Dynamic refers to a value that is determined at runtime and might change over the life of the program such as: int num = someFunction();.

| X | 0 | 1 | 2 | 3 | 4 |
|---|---|---|---|---|---|
|   | ↓ | ↓ | ↓ | ↓ | ↓ |
| Y | 0 | 0 | 0 | 0 | 0 |
|   | 1 | 1 | 1 | 1 | 1 |
|   | 2 | 2 | 2 | 2 | 2 |
|   | 3 | 3 | 3 | 3 | 3 |
|   | 4 | 4 | 4 | 4 | 4 |

Visualization of a 2D array

Arrays are great for fast lookup, which will be important as our Game Board expands. Arrays reserve a portion of memory and assign a call number called an index to every block of memory in the array. This gives the array a fixed size guaranteeing that we won't run into memory problems when generating the world. Also, looking up any index in an array is nearly instant.

The main issue with using a two-dimensional array is that we have to predefine the size. This means that as soon as the game starts, we will reserve a large chunk of memory for our game that we might not use. It is even worse if we end up filling the array before the game is over, as then we have to make a new larger array, transfer all the information to the new array, and deallocate all the memory of the old array.

The larger array then faces the same two problems as described previously. This method also means having to spend extra development time to write the logic that would perform the array rewrite task. Our game might then start to slow down as our memory expands and contracts to make new arrays and delete old ones. This will still be a viable option, but perhaps with a little more careful development work.

# Linked list

The 2D array has the important feature of fast look up but the implementation would be inefficient and it also runs the risk of creating too much overhead. So another option would be a list, which is a form of linked list. The list doesn't need to reserve a chunk of memory because each entry in the list holds a link reference to the entry before it and after it in the list. This means that list entries can be stored anywhere in the memory, which eliminates the need to reserve any memory on startup.

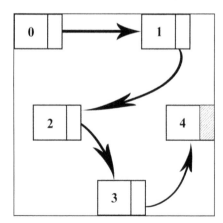

Visualization of a linked list

The list solves the problem of having to create a new array when you run out of space. We can easily and continuously add to a list dynamically, as well. However, the fast look up will suffer slightly with lists and therefore cause the performance of the game to suffer. When an array is created, the structure of it is like a chart where each entry is adjacent to the next and the system can scan very quickly to a specified index. Lists, on the other hand, have entries littered throughout the memory so the system has to start at the first entry and follow each entry to the specified index.

One more caveat of a list is that we wouldn't be able to reference an index that we hadn't already filled with a tile. In our 2D array example, all of the indices of the array are predefined and can be referenced, even though they are empty. List entries don't have place holders like this. If we reference a list entry that doesn't exist, the system will throw an exception and most likely freeze the game if we aren't prepared for it. We would have to predefine all the entries in the list to circumvent this issue, which means a list is little better than an array at this point.

So now we are at the crossroads of choosing the lesser of two evils. In one hand, we have the array that needs some overhead maintenance to add tiles dynamically. On the other hand, we have a list that can be dynamically added to, but we are forced into a similar overhead to maintain our free flowing grid structure. Our ideal data structure can have dynamic entry additions with a fast lookup, but with none of the costs associated with arrays and lists. Again, this is a perfectly viable option, but perhaps there's another that will suit our needs better.

# Dictionary

The compromise is something called a **Dictionary** in C#, which is a form of an associative array. An associative array is just a modified array to use some other data type like a string as the index instead of a non-negative number. The dictionary uses a key-value pair to store data and it can be dynamically added to and removed from. However, keep in mind that the dictionary will continue to take up as much memory as its maximum size. The dictionary key-value pair would look something like this:

```
Dictionary myInventory (string key, int value);
myInventory.Add("Gold", 10);
myInventory["Gold"];
```

The C# dictionary is a class that wraps an array. This class will notice when the internal array is about to become full and will perform the task of rewriting our data into a larger array automatically. The dictionary also has a fast lookup speed. Having an associative array as our data structure also benefits us by only needing to create a one-dimensional array instead of a two-dimensional array as in the previous examples.

Because the dictionary takes a key-value pair, we can make our key a Vector2 with our X and Y coordinates of each placed tile. This way, when we want to know whether a specific tile has been placed already, we can look up the X and Y coordinates directly. The `Dictionary` class has a method called `Contains()` making lookups as easy as `myInventory.Contains("Gold");`. This will give us a `true`/`false` value that we can check in an `if...else` or a `switch` statement.

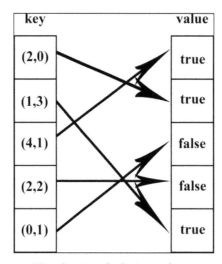

Visualization of a dictionary/map

Here is a summary of our data structure choice:

- **Array**: This is a simple data structure with fast lookup but it is difficult to add tiles dynamically.

- **List**: This is a linked list, which can have tiles added dynamically, but will have slower lookup as the list gets bigger.

- **Dictionary**: This is an associative array class with built-in array resizing and a fast lookup.

  Even though the dictionary has a little more overhead with it's extra class methods, it will be the most efficient data structure for our use. It is also really easy to use.

# PCG algorithm overview

Now that we settled on our data structure for managing our Game Board grid, we need to design our algorithm for placing tiles. This algorithm will use two types of PCG. We will only create tiles that the player discovers, which is a form of player-triggered PCG. We will also use random numbers to dictate the look of the tile and to choose which floor tiles will have a wall tile placed on top.

To start our algorithm design, let's imagine and try to visualize a use case. We want our player to start in a small area that has already been revealed and added to our data structure. When the game starts, let's create a 5 x 5 grid of tiles for an initial Game Board. We can then place our player character in the center of the grid initially.

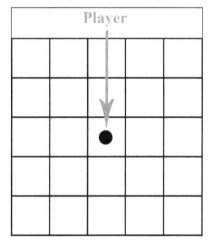

The initial Game Board grid with the player

As the player explores, our algorithm will reveal more tiles in the direction the player is headed. We will refer to this as the player's *line of sight*. We can use any arbitrary number of tiles to reveal ahead of the player. Six tiles feels like a good amount, though. This will give us a center point on which to place the player character.

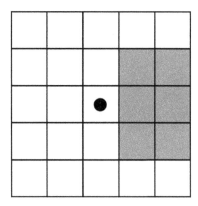

The line of sight grid squares are shaded

Every time the player moves into another tile, we will check the six tiles in front of the character. In order to accomplish this, we will need to track the player's position as a Vector2 with an X and Y coordinate. We will also need to track the direction in which the player is moving. With the player position and direction, we can find the coordinates of the six tiles in front of the player.

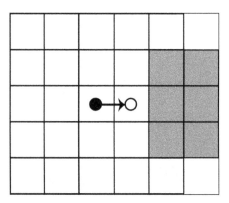

Revealing more tiles as the player moves right

As the player explores and returns to the areas, the six tiles spaces in the player's line of sight might have already been revealed and in our dictionary. So, with every step the player takes, we need to check each of the six lines of sight tiles to see whether the player has already discovered them. If we find that a tile is already in our dictionary, we don't want to overwrite it with a new tile because it might change its look.

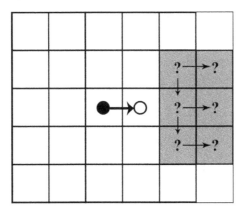

The tiles are iterated over to check whether they have already been discovered

When we check the player's line of sight, we will perform one of two actions on each tile. If the tile is undiscovered, we will add its coordinates to our dictionary, randomly choose a floor tile sprite to place, put it on the Game Board, and randomly add a wall tile on top of the floor tile. Otherwise, if the floor tile is already in our dictionary, we will just ignore it. We have to make sure that we are updating the player's position as well for this algorithm to work.

Here is a summary of our PCG algorithm:

- The player moves one tile in any direction
- Get direction where the player moved
- Update the coordinates of the player's position
- Use the player's position to find and check the 6th line of sight tiles
- Add undiscovered tiles to our dictionary and place them on the Game Board
- Randomly add wall tiles to newly added floor tiles
- Ignore previously discovered tiles

# Scene setup

Now that we chose a data structure and designed our algorithm, we need to set up our scene. At the moment, at the start of our game, the player character shows up in the corner of the screen with a black backdrop. The player can move in four directions but could potentially move off screen. The player can also move under the text that shows the player's health. We should fix this so that we can better see our PCG algorithm in action.

# Player positioning

Previously, we said that a starting grid of 5 x 5 for our initial Game Board would be a good metric. So let's continue with a 5 x 5 Game Board in mind. If our 5 x 5 grid starts with the X-Y coordinate or (0,0) in the lower-left corner and (4,4) in the upper-right corner, then (2,2) will be the center of the grid. Select the **Player** prefab in the **Hierarchy** panel and set both the X and Y values to 2.

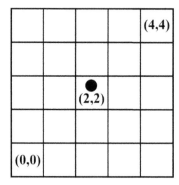

The grid will correspond with the x-y plane

Each sprite in our sprite sheet is 32 x 32 pixels. When the sprite sheet was imported, the Pixels to Units import setting was set to 32 pixels equals 1 Unity unit of measure. So our Game Board will align precisely with the Unity x-y plane. We can then build our Game Board around our player character starting at (0,0) in the lower-left corner. This same unit of measure will be used to track our player's position.

All our sprites are 32 x 32, which is 1 unit of measure

We changed the position of the player character, but that doesn't prevent the player from being able to walk off screen. We need a way to keep the player character in sight at all times. We can write a script that makes it possible for the player to only move as far as the screen edge but that doesn't make sense since our Game Board is infinite. Instead, we can have the camera move with the player.

# Camera following

Unity makes it easy to have a camera follow the player. There is a script in the Unity Standard Assets called `Camera2DFollow.cs`. We will simply import the script, which is included when you download Unity. We can then adjust the settings to suit our needs.

To import the script, follow these steps:

1. In the top menu, navigate to **Assets** | **Import Package** | **2D**.
2. In the **Importing package** popup, select **None** to uncheck all the options.
3. Find and check the `Camera2DFollow.cs` package by navigating to the **2D** | **Scripts** directory.
4. Click on **Import**.

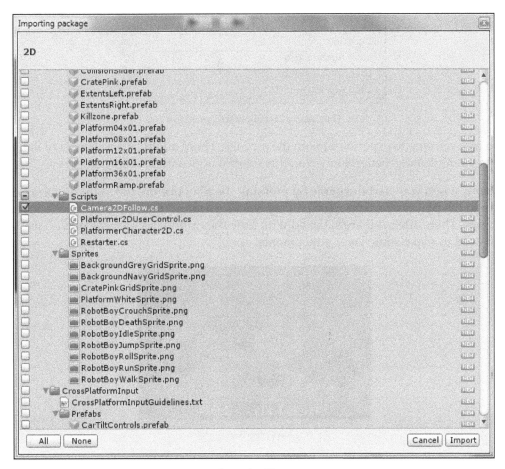

Import settings

You will have a **Standard Assets** folder added to your project. Inside the **Standard Assets** folder is **2D | Scripts | Camera2DFollow.cs**. Drag and drop the **Camera2DFollow** script onto the **Main Camera**. Then, from the **Hierarchy** pane, drag and drop the **Player** prefab onto the **Target** field in the **Camera2DFollow** script component of the **Main Camera**.

We are going to change the other settings as well:

- Set the **Damping** field to 1
- Set the **Look Ahead Factor** field to 1
- Set the **Look Ahead Return Speed** field to 0.5
- Set the **Look Ahead Move Threshold** field to 0.1

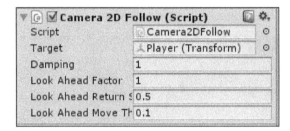

The Camera 2D Follow settings screen

You are welcome to experiment with the settings. There might be another set of values that you think looks better. However, this setup works without being too jerky.

So now, when you start the game by pressing the play button, the Main Camera will snap to the player character. You can try walking around to test the camera follow settings. Then, after you are satisfied with how the camera follows the player, we will need to make some layer adjustments.

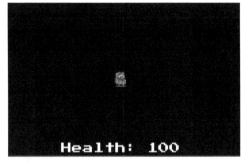

No Game Board

# Layers

Even though our game is 2D and takes place on only one visible plane, we can still place game objects on different layers to manage how things interact. So, we will add some layers to manage how the player interacts with their environment:

- Select the **Player** prefab from the **Hierarchy** panel

- Select the **Layer** field dropdown

- Select **Add Layer...** from the dropdown

- Add `BlockingLayer`, `Floor`, and `Units` as layer labels to any empty field (do not overwrite any existing field)

- Then, select the **Sorting Layers** dropdown on the same screen

- Add `Floor` and `Units` as **Sorting Layer** labels, in that order

 These layers might have been added from the import process in *Chapter 2, Roguelike Games* but this is not guaranteed.

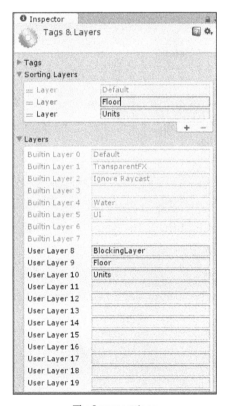

The Layer settings

The layers will help us divide tiles into specific regions of interest. Game objects that are impassable or can prevent the player from moving will be placed on the BlockingLayer. The **Player** prefab and wall tiles will be on the BlockingLayer because the player should not simply be able to walk through walls.

The sorting layer is important because it will dictate which sprites are rendered first. We want the player character to render on top of the floor tiles. The layers at the top of the **Sorting Layers** list are rendered first. So we place the Floor layer higher in the list so that it is rendered before the player character.

Now, we have to select the **Layer** and **Sorting Layer** in the **Sprite Renderer** component of our **Player** prefab, floor tiles, and wall tiles.

For the **Player** prefab, follow these steps:

1.   In the **Hierarchy** panel, select **Player**.
2.   Select the **Layer** dropdown.
3.   Select **BlockingLayer**.
4.   In the **Sprite Renderer** component, select the **Sorting Layer** dropdown.
5.   Select **Units**.

For the floor tiles, follow these steps:

1.   In the **Project** tab, select the **Prefabs** folder.
2.   Select **Floor1** to **Floor8** at the same time using the *Shift* or *command* key.
3.   In the **Sprite Renderer** component, select the **Sorting Layer** dropdown.
4.   Select **Floor**.

For the wall tiles, follow these steps:

1.   In the **Project** tab, select the **Prefabs** folder.
2.   Select **Wall1** to **Wall8** at the same time.
3.   Select the **Layer** dropdown.
4.   Select **BlockingLayer**.
5.   In the **Sprite Renderer** component, select the **Sorting Layer** dropdown.
6.   Select **Units**.

Unfortunately, layers in Unity do not carry over when making a package of your project. The reasoning behind this is that you might have created some layers in your project and then imported a package. If the imported package brought along it's layers, it might overwrite some of your originally created layers. For more on layers, visit the Unity Docs at http://docs.unity3d.com/Manual/Layers.html.

# Initial Game Board

Now that we have our algorithm designed and the Unity Editor setup, we can start our code implementation. We'll approach the task in small pieces. First, let's put down a small starting area for our player. As stated before, we will make a 5 x 5 grid to lay floor tiles on. The lower-left corner will be placed at (0,0) and the upper-right corner at (4,4) with the player character at (2,2).

We'll start by building our BoardManager class. Open up BoardManager.cs for editing. Currently, there is only a public class called Count, but we are about to change that. *Code Snip 3.1* shows the additions we want to make to BoardManager.cs:

```
1 using UnityEngine;
2 using System;
3 using System.Collections.Generic;
4 using Random = UnityEngine.Random;
5
6 public class BoardManager : MonoBehaviour {
7   [Serializable]
8   public class Count {
9     public int minimum;
10    public int maximum;
11
12    public Count (int min, int max) {
13      minimum = min;
14      maximum = max;
15    }
16  }
17
18  public int columns = 5;
19  public int rows = 5;
20  public GameObject[] floorTiles;
21  private Transform boardHolder;
22  private Dictionary<Vector2, Vector2> gridPositions = new
      Dictionary<Vector2, Vector2> ();
```

```
23
24   public void BoardSetup () {
25   boardHolder = new GameObject ("Board").transform;
26
27   for(int x = 0; x < columns; x++) {
28     for(int y = 0; y < rows; y++) {
29       gridPositions.Add(new Vector2(x,y), new Vector2(x,y));
30
31       GameObject toInstantiate = floorTiles[Random.Range
         (0,floorTiles.Length)];
32
33       GameObject instance = Instantiate (toInstantiate, new
         Vector3 (x, y, 0f), Quaternion.identity) as GameObject;
34
35       instance.transform.SetParent (boardHolder);
36     }
37   }
38 }
39 }
```

So our original BoardManager class has doubled in size. Let's take a look at what we added:

- Line 18-19: Here are two public integer variables called row and column, which represent our starting Game Board grid.

- Line 20: floorTiles is a public GameObject array that will hold all the floor prefabs.

- Line 21: boardHolder is a private transform that will hold all the tiles.

- Line 22: gridPositions is a private dictionary, which is our chosen data structure to hold the list of references to every tile our game lays out.

- Line 24-39: BoardSetup is a public function that returns void. This function will create our initial Game Board and add the tile references to our dictionary.

- Line 27-28: This for loop nested within another for loop will iterate over every cell in our initial 5 x 5 grid.

- Line 31: toInstantiate will randomly choose a tile from our array of floor tiles.

- Line 33: instance will instantiate our randomly chosen floor tile and lay it at the coordinates provided by the for loops.

- Line 35: Finally, we make the instance of the floor tile a child of boardHolder, our Game Board transform.

So, our Game Board is able to set up an initial 5 x 5 board, but the functionality isn't fully integrated yet. We need to make some adjustments to our `GameManager` script as well. We can see the changes needed in *Code Snip 3.2*. Keep in mind that *Code Snip 3.2* is not the full file:

```
 7 public class GameManager : MonoBehaviour {
 8
 9   public float turnDelay = 0.1f;
10   public int healthPoints = 100;
11   public static GameManager instance = null;
12   [HideInInspector] public bool playersTurn = true;
13
14   private BoardManager boardScript;
15   private List<Enemy> enemies;
16   private bool enemiesMoving;
17
18   void Awake() {
19     if (instance == null)
20       instance = this;
21     else if (instance != this)
22       Destroy(gameObject);
23
24     DontDestroyOnLoad(gameObject);
25
26     enemies = new List<Enemy>();
27
28     boardScript = GetComponent<BoardManager>();
29
30     InitGame();
31   }
...
56   void InitGame() {
57     enemies.Clear();
58
59     boardScript.BoardSetup();
60 }
```

There's only a few key lines here to integrate the `BoardManager` class with the rest of the game. Let's see what the changes are:

- Line 14: `boardScript` is the variable we will use to keep a reference to our `BoardManager` script.

- Line 28: Inside the `Awake` function, we will have `boardScript` reference the `BoardManager` script that we will add to our `GameManager` prefab.

- `Line 59`: Inside the `InitGame` function, we will call the `BoardSetup` function from our attached `BoardManager` script.

So, now the `BoardManager` script functionality will be called from the `GameManager` script. However, when you press play, there is still no Game Board. We are still missing a few connections, which we will need to set up in the Unity Editor.

In the **Project** tab, follow these steps:

1. Select the **Prefabs** folder.
2. Select the **GameManager** prefab.
3. In the **Inspector** tab, select the **Add Component** button.
4. From the **Add Component** dropdown, navigate to **Script | BoardManager**.

These steps add the `BoardManager` script to our **GameManager** prefab, but we need to add the floor tile references now.

In the **Board Manager** script component of the **GameManager** prefab, follow these steps:

1. Set **Size** under **Floor Tiles** to 8 and press *Enter*.
2. Then, drag and drop **Floor1** to **Floor8** into the newly created **Element0** to **Element7** under **Floor Tiles**.

Now, we can press the play button and we'll see our player character standing on our initial 5 x 5 Game Board. Notice that because our initial Game Board is procedurally generated, it is made up of a different combination of tiles every time we play the game. However, this isn't the end of our PCG game world. We want the Game Board to expand as the player explores.

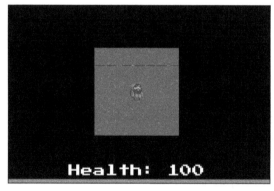

Initial Game Board

# Connecting code

We now need to add the functionality of our expanding Game Board. As per our algorithm design, we need to track the player character's position. When the player moves, we need to send the player character's position and direction to the BoardManager class. So let's start with the additions needed in the Player script shown in *Code Snip 3.3*:

```
7 public class Player : MovingObject {
8    public int wallDamage = 1;
9    public Text healthText;
10   private Animator animator;
11   private int health;
12   public static Vector2 position;
13
14   protected override void Start () {
15
16     animator = GetComponent<Animator>();
17
18     health = GameManager.instance.healthPoints;
19
20     healthText.text = "Health: " + health;
21
22     position.x = position.y = 2;
23
24     base.Start ();
25   }
26   private void Update () {
27     if(!GameManager.instance.playersTurn) return;
28
29     int horizontal = 0;
30     int vertical = 0;
31
32     bool canMove = false;
33
34     horizontal = (int) (Input.GetAxisRaw ("Horizontal"));
35     vertical = (int) (Input.GetAxisRaw ("Vertical"));
36
37     if(horizontal != 0)
38     {
39       vertical = 0;
40     }
41     if(horizontal != 0 || vertical != 0)
42     {
```

```
43          canMove = AttemptMove<Wall> (horizontal, vertical);
44          if(canMove) {
45            position.x += horizontal;
46            position.y += vertical;
47            GameManager.instance.updateBoard(horizontal, vertical);
48          }
49       }
50    }
51
52    protected override bool AttemptMove <T> (int xDir, int yDir) {
53       bool hit = base.AttemptMove <T> (xDir, yDir);
54
55       GameManager.instance.playersTurn = false;
56
57       return hit;
58    }
```

In *Code Snip 3.3*, we are changing some of the structure of our base code. These changes will force us to change how some other functions operate. So let's see the new changes and how they'll affect the rest of our development:

- Line 12: position is a public static Vector2 that will hold the current coordinates of our player. It is static so that we can access this variable from any script in the game.

- Line 22: We set the x and y value of position to 2 because we know that at the start of the game, the player character will always begin on (2,2) of our Game Board.

- Line 32: We create a Boolean variable called canMove, which will tell us whether the player is blocked from moving or not. We will calculate this value at every update so it is set to false by default.

- Line 43: Here, we set canMove equal to our AttemptMove function. However, AttemptMove returns void so this will be something we need to fix coming up.

- Line 45-46: position is updated by adding in the values we obtain for horizontal and vertical. horizontal and vertical come from Input. GetAxisRaw, which returns 1 if the player moves in the positive direction or -1 if the player moves in the negative direction.

- Line 47: We call our instance of the GameManager class and invoke the updateBoard function, which doesn't yet exist. We will put this here as a place holder and write the updateBoard function later.

- Line 52: We need to rewrite AttemptMove to return a bool. We will start by declaring that the function will return bool.

- `Line 53`: We are going to create a Boolean variable to hold the bool that `base.AttemptMove` will return. This again is a place holder as `base.AttemptMove` does not yet return a bool. We also need to remove `RaycastHit2D hit`.

- `Line 57`: Return the newly created bool value.

We are using a public static variable for the player position so that we can access it from anywhere at anytime. It is, however, a best practice to make these types of values private and accessible through a `get` function. Having a variable be public static means it can also be changed from anywhere in the code.

This can cause problems if you have more than one person working on a single code base and another developer using the public static variable in a way you didn't intend. It is best to be very deliberate in your code. By forcing a variable to be private and only accessible via a `get` function, you protect the variable from changing in a way that it shouldn't.

With that said, we are going to use the player position as a public static because it is easier and makes our code less bloated. Of course, you are encouraged to revise the code later to make this variable private.

At this point, there are going to be some errors in the Unity Editor because of some conflicts we created. So let's work on clearing the errors. Once everything is working again, we can work on the new functionality.

First, we should fix our bool return value conflict in the `AttemptMove` function of the `MovingObject` class. Remember, `MovingObject` is the base class for both `Player` and `Enemy`. We will have to adjust the `AttemptMove` function in all three files, as it is a `virtual` function.

Let's start by fixing the `AttemptMove` function of `MovingObject`. Open `MovingObject.cs` for editing. *Code Snip 3.4* shows the changes that need to be made to the file:

```
91 protected virtual bool AttemptMove <T> (int xDir, int yDir)
92   where T : Component
93 {
94  RaycastHit2D hit;
95
96  bool canMove = Move (xDir, yDir, out hit);
97
98  if(hit.transform == null)
99    return true;
```

```
100
101 T hitComponent = hit.transform.GetComponent <T> ();
102
103 if(!canMove && hitComponent != null)
104   OnCantMove (hitComponent);
105
106 return false;
107 }
```

We only need to adjust the one function within the MovingObject class. Let's take a look at how it changed in *Code Snip 3.4*:

- Line 91: We need to change the void return type to bool
- Line 99: Return the bool value as true if the player hit an object
- Line 106: Return false if we reached the end of the function, meaning that the player didn't hit anything

If you return to the Unity Editor, you should see some new errors. One will be complaining that the Enemy class has implemented AttemptMove incorrectly. So let's address this next.

Our Enemy class at the moment is only a place holder. If you remember from *Chapter 2, Roguelike Games*, we are using the Enemy class as a way to dictate movement turns. Because our game is turn based, we need the player to wait for each visible enemy to move before the player can move again. The base code has implemented a scan for enemies, each turn using the Enemy class place holder so we won't have to do it later.

So the adjustment to the Enemy class is fairly simple. *Code Snip 3.5* shows the changes:

```
6 protected override bool AttemptMove <T> (int xDir, int yDir)
7 {
8   return true;
9 }
```

The explanation for *Code Snip 3.5* is equally simple. Keep in mind though that this is still a place holder class and we will do a full implementation later on. Let's take a look at the changes made:

- Line 6: The return type is changed from void to bool.
- Line 8: Return true so that we are returning the correct value at the end of the function. We need to return a bool value at the end of the function so the compiler will pass this as a nonerror. However, the bool value doesn't matter as it is not used yet.

We are almost done mending our code. We have one more error to handle before we put in our expanding Game Board functionality. Returning to the Unity Editor yet again will reveal that we called a function (that doesn't exist) from the Player class to the GameManager class. We need to add the updateBoard function to the GameManager class as a connection from the Player class to the BoardManager class.

Add *Code Snip 3.6* at the end of your GameManager definition:

```
public void updateBoard (int horizantal, int vertical) {}
```

updateBoard is called from the Player class whenever the player makes a successful move. Since updateBoard is a method of the GameManager class, we can call a public method of the BoardManager class here. We will use this connection to develop our PCG Game Board functionality.

# The PCG Game Board

We are all set to write the core functionality of our PCG Game Board. The goal is to have tiles laid out in the direction the player character walks. We designed our algorithm in such a way that the Game Board will expand as the player explores.

We connected our scripts so that when the player moves, the Player class will update the player position and send it to the GameManager class. The GameManager class will then call a method in the BoardManager class to update the Game Board and pass along the player position and direction. We now need to write the code that will update the Game Board based on the player position.

Let's start by adding the function that will update the Game Board in the BoardManager class. Open up BoardManager.cs for editing. *Code Snip 3.7* shows the function that needs to be added:

```
77 public void addToBoard (int horizontal, int vertical) {
78   if (horizontal == 1) {
79     //Check if tiles exist
80     int x = (int)Player.position.x;
81     int sightX = x + 2;
82     for (x += 1; x <= sightX; x++) {
83       int y = (int)Player.position.y;
84       int sightY = y + 1;
85       for (y -= 1; y <= sightY; y++) {
86         addTiles(new Vector2 (x, y));
87       }
88     }
89 }
```

```
 90   else if (horizontal == -1) {
 91     int x = (int)Player.position.x;
 92     int sightX = x - 2;
 93     for (x -= 1; x >= sightX; x--) {
 94       int y = (int)Player.position.y;
 95       int sightY = y + 1;
 96       for (y -= 1; y <= sightY; y++) {
 97         addTiles(new Vector2 (x, y));
 98       }
 99     }
100   }
101   else if (vertical == 1) {
102     int y = (int)Player.position.y;
103     int sightY = y + 2;
104     for (y += 1; y <= sightY; y++) {
105       int x = (int)Player.position.x;
106       int sightX = x + 1;
107       for (x -= 1; x <= sightX; x++) {
108         addTiles(new Vector2 (x, y));
109       }
110     }
111   }
112   else if (vertical == -1) {
113     int y = (int)Player.position.y;
114     int sightY = y - 2;
115     for (y -= 1; y >= sightY; y--) {
116       int x = (int)Player.position.x;
117       int sightX = x + 1;
118       for (x -= 1; x <= sightX; x++) {
119         addTiles(new Vector2 (x, y));
120       }
121     }
122   }
123 }
```

This function contains a switch driven by direction. The base code is set up to return only one directional value at a time. This means our player character can only move one direction at a time. Either the player moves horizontally in the positive or negative $x$ direction forcing the vertical direction to return 0, or vice versa along the $y$ direction.

Let's take a closer look at the code:

- Line 77: addToBoard is a public function returning void. This will be our entry point from the GameManager class. From the GameManager class, we pass the player direction to this function as arguments.

- Line 78: This is our first switch point. If horizontal equals 1, then we know vertical is 0. This corresponds to the player moving to the right on screen.

- Line 80-85: We are using a for loop nested within a for loop to iterate over the player's line of sight. Remember the line of sight is the six tile spaces directly in front of the player's movement direction. The line of sight makes up a 2 x 3 grid.

- Line 86: For each tile space we iterate over, we will call the method addTiles and pass in the Vector2 produced by our for loops. addTiles does not exist yet but we will be writing it next.

- Line 90-122: The rest of the function is simply a variation of Lines 78-86. If the player did not move to the right, then we check the other directions and set up the line of sight for that direction.

Next, we will complete our expanding Game Board functionality by writing the addTiles function used in the addToBoard function you just wrote. The main objective of this function is to check our dictionary for the line of sight tiles and if they are not there, we add them. *Code Snip 3.8* shows the function as part of the BoardManager class:

```
61 private void addTiles(Vector2 tileToAdd) {
62   if (!gridPositions.ContainsKey (tileToAdd)) {
63     gridPositions.Add (tileToAdd, tileToAdd);
64     GameObject toInstantiate = floorTiles [Random.Range (0,
       floorTiles.Length)];
65     GameObject instance = Instantiate (toInstantiate, new
       Vector3 (tileToAdd.x, tileToAdd.y, 0f), Quaternion.identity)
       as GameObject;
66
67     instance.transform.SetParent (boardHolder);
68   }
69 }
```

This code should seem familiar. We do similar calls in the `BoardSetup` function of the `BoardManager` class. `Line 62` is the main difference. Here, we check the dictionary for the tile before we proceed. If the tile is in the dictionary, we return out of the function. This prevents us from overwriting tiles that have already been placed in the game.

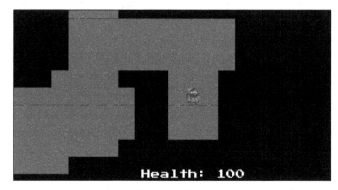

PCG Game Board

You can now return to the Unity Editor and test the new functionality. Click on the play button to try it out. As per our algorithm design, whenever the player moves, more tiles are revealed in that direction.

This Game Board isn't very interesting, though. We can walk in a single direction forever with no opposition. This terrain would also make it very easy to run away from enemies. We should add some wall tiles for obstacles.

Let's return to editing the `BoardManager.cs` file. We are going to add onto our `addTiles` function by putting in a condition that adds wall tiles to newly placed floor tiles. *Code Snip 3.9* shows the code addition:

```
29 public GameObject[] wallTiles;
...
62 private void addTiles(Vector2 tileToAdd) {
63  if (!gridPositions.ContainsKey (tileToAdd)) {
64     gridPositions.Add (tileToAdd, tileToAdd);
65     GameObject toInstantiate = floorTiles [Random.Range (0,
        floorTiles.Length)];
66     GameObject instance = Instantiate (toInstantiate, new
        Vector3 (tileToAdd.x, tileToAdd.y, 0f), Quaternion.identity)
        as GameObject;
```

```
67
68      instance.transform.SetParent (boardHolder);
69
70        //Choose at random a wall tile to lay
71      if (Random.Range (0, 3) == 1) {
72        toInstantiate = wallTiles[Random.Range (0,wallTiles.Length)];
        instance = Instantiate (toInstantiate, new Vector3
        (tileToAdd.x, tileToAdd.y, 0f), Quaternion.identity) as
        GameObject;
73        instance.transform.SetParent (boardHolder);
74      }
75  }
76 }
```

Let's take a look at what we added in *Code Snip 3.9*:

- `Line 29`: Like the floor tiles, we are going to add an array of `GameObject` to hold our wall tile prefabs.
- `Line 62-68`: This is our original `addTiles` function.
- `Line 71`: This condition uses random numbers to create a probability. We randomly choose a number between 0 and 2. If the number is 1, then we add a wall tile to the newly created floor tile. There is a 1 in 3 or 33 percent chance that a wall tile is added.
- Line 72-74: We instantiate the wall tiles as we do the floor tiles.

So, if we return to the Unity Editor and play the game, we get some errors. This is because we added the array for the wall tiles, but it is currently empty. You will need to add the wall tiles to the `GameManager` prefab the same way you did the floor tiles.

In the `BoardManager` script component of the `GameManager` prefab, follow these steps:

1. Set **Size** under **Wall Tiles** to 8 and press *Enter*.
2. Then, drag and drop **Wall1** to **Wall8** into the newly created **Element0** to **Element7** under **Wall Tiles**.

Finally, the Game Board is fully functional! Press the play button to test it out. The Game Board will expand as the player explores. Every time you play the game, you will experience a different Game Board.

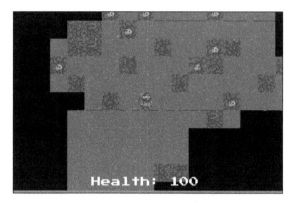

PCG Game Board plus wall tiles

With the addition of high frequency wall spawning, there are plenty of obstacles. These walls will also make it more difficult to run from enemies. The PCG nature of the Game Board makes for a unique play of the game every time.

# Summary

Our *Roguelike* game is coming along. You completed your first PCG feature from design to development. However, there is still plenty left to do.

In this chapter, you learned about and analyzed a few different data structures. You designed an algorithm that will expand the Game Board as the player explores. You set up the scene so we could implement our PCG algorithm by adding layers and a player tracking camera feature. And finally, you implemented our algorithm design and created a procedurally generated game world.

There's still more game world to procedurally generate. In the next chapter, we are going to develop a different kind of level building. We will be creating a random dungeon generator. This will present a new set of PCG algorithm challenges.

# 4

# Generating Random Dungeons

Our PCG *Roguelike* game is developing nicely. In the previous chapter, we produced a game board that expanded as the player explored the game. We are going to continue with the game board idea with a new type of board, the Dungeon Board. We will thus refer to our initial game board as the world board. The world board will be persistent and lead the player to instances of Dungeon Boards. Though we could add many different game mechanics to the world board alone, we want to learn more of what PCG has to offer. In this chapter, we want to explore another type of PCG level creation. We are going to make a random dungeon generator.

Our world board is a type of player-driven PCG. The world board reveals the pieces of board that the player dictates. Our dungeon generator will be system driven. We will develop an algorithm to completely create a whole dungeon. Using PRNs, we will allow randomness to dictate the shape and size of our dungeon.

By not controlling too much of our dungeon generator, we should get some surprisingly unique and interesting dungeon designs. However, we will have to provide some guidelines. Random events can add fun and spontaneity, but that same spontaneity can be unwieldy and either overwhelm the player or cause problems within the system such as building paths off the defined area bounds.

Image of final result of dungeon generator

Here's what you can expect from this chapter:

- Learn a system-driven PCG algorithm
- Explore the uses of queues
- Manipulate PRNs to create random events
- Develop a random dungeon generator
- Return to the idea of seeding PRNs to recreate patterns

Now, let's jump into how to develop a dungeon generator.

# Algorithm design

In order to successfully design an algorithm for a randomly generated dungeon, we need to define what we mean by *dungeon*. In video games, a dungeon is typically an enclosed labyrinth-like level with a start and an end. A subgenre of games called a **dungeon crawler** gets its name from having the player complete many of these levels known as dungeons. *Roguelike* games are also known for their dungeon crawler style game play but with the extension that the dungeons are procedurally generated.

So our aim is to make a maze-like level layout and design. There are plenty of maze creating algorithms that are well defined and documented on the Internet. You should spend some time looking at some of these maze creation algorithms and trying to understand them. However, we will be writing our own algorithm to get the most exposure to the topic.

# Algorithm overview

We can create the dungeon, much like we do the game world board. We will lay out tiles representing the floor for our player to walk on. However, the difference is that we need to enclose the dungeon board, making it finite, and contain the player within bounds. And thus, we can add an entrance and an exit to the dungeon level as the only means in and out.

The game world is generated continuously as the player explores. This won't work for our dungeon as it needs a start and an end. We will have to generate the entire dungeon at once. This isn't always the case, but this will best suit our needs for this task. In this respect, there is a bit of game/level design that can happen when developing these algorithms to achieve the look and feel you desire for the level.

There are many ways we can do this. One of the most popular ways is to place large sections of predefined dungeon and connect them together. However, predefining sections of dungeon would force us to do more art creation than coding. In your own projects, the choice is yours to make. But for this project, what we can do is use **pathfinding** to create a way though our dungeon, and then add procedurally generated sections of dungeon onto that path.

# The grid

Pathfinding is usually applied to a map, graph, or some other structure that has separated points. We think of our world board as a grid that is just a graph of points on the x-y plane. We can do the same with our Dungeon Board. Using the grid concept, we will inherently know all the points in our dungeon.

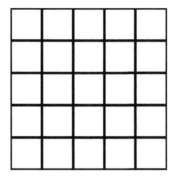

A diagram of the simple grid

We can then guide our algorithm and keep it within the bounds of the grid. So, if we imagine our dungeon grid as a square grid, we can pick a start point on the left somewhere. Then, we use some pathfinding to find its way to the right and place an endpoint. We can record every point the pathfinder took on the grid and place tiles there. The result is the start of a random dungeon.

There are some very well-defined pathfinding algorithms in computer science, but we will create our own for our dungeon. However, you should always research a new topic and find out more about it on your own. Pathfinding is an important part of game development and has many uses.

Note: Path-finding is used in most videos game. There are some situations where a character will follow a predefined path, but in most instances of gameplay, we need the AI to adapt to dynamic changes. *Dijkstra's Algorithm* is a basis for path finding and is studied in general in most computer science academic programs. A general search on Dijkstra's Algorithm and pathfinding will yield a wealth of information. Even more relevant to game development is a path finding algorithm called **A***, which you should also research.

Usually, pathfinding is meant to find the shortest/easiest path through an area to a destination. Because of their complexity, most pathfinding algorithms will be over-qualified for our task. We are looking to be a little surprised of the outcome ourselves, so we want to develop an algorithm that is based on randomness and is not so directed.

We want our pathfinder to be spontaneous because that will translate to a more interesting dungeon layout. We only want the dimensions of the grid to contain the pathfinder. However, the pathfinder will require some direction in the form of random probability.

# Essential path

If we were to randomly lay tiles on our grid for our dungeon, we could end up with a dungeon that doesn't connect and has an entrance but with an inaccessible exit. So we can utilize as much of the grid as possible to create our entrance on the far left and our exit on the far right. Then, we connect the two with our pathfinder, which we will call the **essential path**.

The essential path is just that, essential. By connecting the entrance to the exit, we ensure our dungeon can be completed. All the points on the essential path will have a floor tile to make sure the path is open. We can then add to the essential path to expand the dungeon.

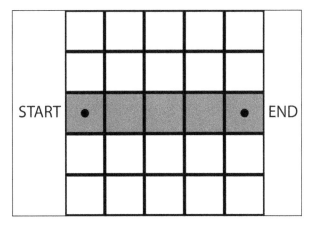

A diagram of the simplest essential path

The simplest path in a grid or point system is a straight line. However, a straight line for a dungeon isn't very interesting. So we should guide our path from left to right but use some PRNs to create a probability that it veers up or down. This should give us a nice winding path.

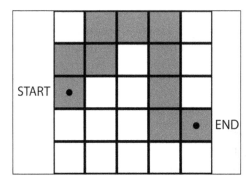

A diagram of the winding essential path

# Random path and chambers

Once we have created our essential path, we can add to it. This will add even more variety to our dungeon and ensure that no two are alike during game play. We will call these random branches from the essential path, **random paths**.

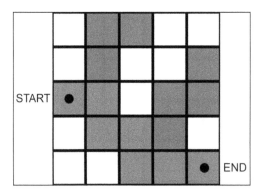

A diagram of random paths in blue

We can further add to a random path by placing a large opening at the end, which we will call a **chamber**. The chamber mimics the type of dungeon generation we spoke of earlier in which we predefine sections of the dungeon and place them in. However, instead of predefining the chambers by building them as an art asset, we will build the chambers procedurally. This will ensure that they will fit anywhere in our grid, as well as save us some memory by not having to store one or more chamber types as art assets.

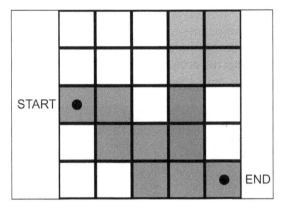

A diagram of the chamber in red

# Filling in the rest of the gird

After placing the essential paths, random paths, and chambers, we will have a set of coordinates that refers to open space. This open space will be the floor tiles of the Dungeon Board. We then need to enclose the dungeon or we will be able to walk into the blank region of the screen.

We can easily do this but filling in the rest of the grid with tiles that the player cannot move on or through. These tiles are wall tiles that cannot be destroyed by the player. These tiles are called outer wall tiles and they were already added to your prefab set as of *Chapter 2, Roguelike Games.*

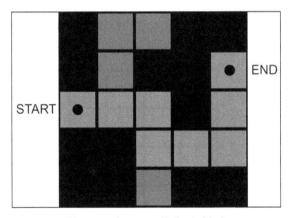

Diagram of outer wall tiles in black

Also, since we are moving from the far left to the far right, we will be placing tiles on the very edge of the Dungeon Board grid. This will create an opening to the blank space onscreen. The same can happen to any random path that makes it to the end of the grid. So, we should wrap the entire grind in a single tile width of outer wall tiles to make sure the dungeon is truly closed.

A diagram of the outer wall tiles enclosing the dungeon in black

# Placing the entrance and exit

Finally, we need to define how the entrance and exit are determined in the dungeon. Even though we are discussing this last, it will actually be the first thing the algorithm does. We already decided that we will be moving from left to right. From the far left of the grid, we can randomly select a point by varying the $y$ coordinate. So, we know our entrance will have an $x$ coordinate of **0** and a random $y$ coordinate.

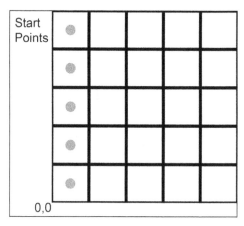

A diagram of possible starting points

After defining the entrance, we can have the path build off of the starting point. However, the path is unpredictable and it will be difficult to try and have it connect with a specified end point. Instead, we can let the path-finder run its course knowing that it will find its way to the far right side. We will then take the point at which the path ends itself, that is, the exit of the dungeon.

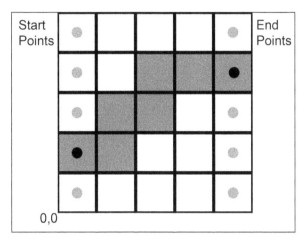

A diagram of the placement of exit based on the path

# Algorithm summary

Algorithms, like this one, can get long and complicated when trying to determine how and when to branch the path. To avoid complexity, we will let PRNs create a probability for certain outcomes. This way, we can leave the branching up to chance. Thus, our algorithm will be doing most of the level layout but we have some idea of the flow of the level based on our algorithm design. Let's summarize our algorithm:

- Set up the grid if we use a square grid; then, we only need to store a single number, which will represent all four sides, say 5 for a 5 x 5 grid.

- Generate the essential path from left to right, which will connect the dungeon entrance to the dungeon exit.

  We can use a PRN here to determine the direction the path takes.

- Add random path branches to the essential path.

  This is another opportunity to use PRNs as a probability of a branch creation and also to determine the direction it takes.

- Fill in the rest of the grid with impassable wall tiles to enclose the dungeon, which is inefficient but easy. You are welcome to trim the wall tiles to only surround the path and are encouraged to do so.

# Data structures

Now that we know the instruction set of our dungeon creation, we need to figure out how we plan to store the dungeon board. We are building the Dungeon Board in a similar manner that we built the world board, so we might be able to use similar data structures. There are enough differences though, that we will need to evaluate what works best.

# Back to the map

We are using a dictionary to store our world board because it has an easy and fast lookup method, plus it can be added to dynamically. For all those same reasons, we can use a dictionary to store the important points in our dungeon. Remember, we don't need to know every point in the dungeon, we only need to know the essential and random paths.

The tricky part is that we need to place the essential path first but then revisit every point in the path to potentially add a random branch. There is the option to iterate over the dictionary where we are storing our dungeon. However, we will be adding new points to the dictionary and will need to iterate over those as well. The reason being, a random branch from the essential path can continue on in its own direction.

A random path can move off in any direction and possibly circle back by itself. This would add two of the same entries to our dictionary but our dictionary requires every entry to be unique, which means we cannot have two of the same entry. We want to allow this circling and possible branching of already declared random paths because that's going to give us more possible dungeons variations.

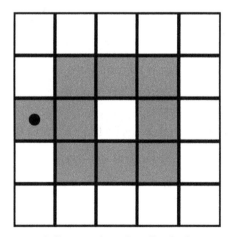

A diagram of a path cycling back

# Queue

So we need a data structure that will allow identical entries but also keep track of where and when to branch. This is a good situation to employ a **Queue**. A queue is an array or list that we populate with entries in some order and then remove those entries in some order. This works for us because we can add a point into the queue that may branch, add the branch point, and then remove the original point so we don't revisit it. To do this, we will be using a queue access and processing called **FIFO**.

FIFO stands for **first in first out**. What this means is that when we add a point to the queue, it will go to the end of the line. The first entry in the queue will be processed and removed, and the next point in the list will take the first spot. This will happen till the list is empty. This is very similar to standing in a line at a bank.

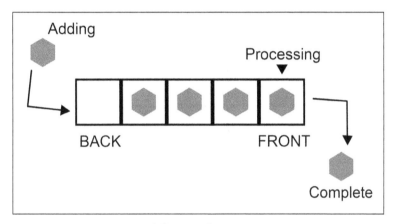

A diagram of a queue

So, let's go over how the queue will operate for our dungeon:

- Once our essential path is created, we can add the points (entrance to exit) to the queue

- We will then process in FIFO

  If a point randomly branches, then we will add that point to the end of the queue

- Whether the point branches or not, it will be removed from the queue and we will process the next point in line

- Eventually, we will process all of the essential path points and begin processing the random paths in the same manner

- This will repeat until no more random paths have been created

Diagram of essential path in queue

Our algorithm and data structures have been finalized. We are ready to start implementing. We just need to set a few things up in the Unity editor before we start.

# Prefab setup

There is some setup that we will need to perform in the Unity editor. We will be making a new prefab. We will continue adding to the *Roguelike* project we have been building from *Chapters 2, Roguelike Games* and *Chapter 3, Generating an Endless World*, so continue from the same project and scene.

The one thing our dungeon design lacks at the moment is a way in and a way out. We need to create a doorway so the player knows where they can enter a dungeon. Likewise, while in a dungeon, we need the same kind of door to signify an exit.

# An exit sign

In the sprite sheet that was initially loaded with the base code during *Chapters 2,
Roguelike Games*, we have a sprite of an exit sign. We can use this same sprite as
both an entrance to the dungeon and an exit from it to save us time. You can easily
change the artwork later if you wish or if you are not using the base game assets,
you can just follow along in how we build the prefab.

Image of exit tile sprite

So let's make a prefab from the exit sign art as the floor and wall tiles:

1.  From the top menu, navigate to **GameObject | Create Empty**.

2.  Select the new empty object in the **Hierarchy** panel.

3.  Name the object Exit.

4.  Add the tag **Exit**.

5.  Select the **Add Component** button in the **Inspector** tab and add the **Sprite
    Renderer** and **Box Collider 2D** components.

6.  In the **Sprite** field of the **Sprite Renderer** component, select **Scavangers_
    SpriteSheet_20**.

7. In the **Sorting Layer** field of the **Sprite Renderer** component, add a new sorting layer **Items**. **Items** should come after **Floor** but before **Units**:

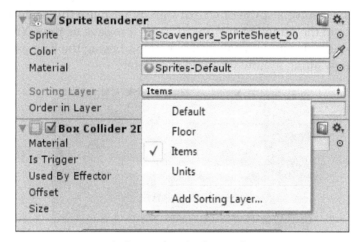

An image of sorting layer order

8. In the **Box Collider 2D** component, check **Is Trigger**.

9. Drag and drop the **Exit** prefab from the **Hierarchy** panel to the **Prefabs** folder.

10. Delete the **Exit** prefab from the **Hierarchy** panel.

This completes the setup for our doorway to and from our dungeons. We will refer the exit tile in code as we implement the dungeon generator. We are going to build a new class around the dungeon generation.

# DungeonManager

Our dungeon generator class will be called DungeonManager. The class will create the data the dungeon is made of and pass it to the BoardManager class to be built on screen. First, we need to create the C# script. Go to the Scripts folder and create a new C# script called DungeonManager.cs.

DungeonManager is a fairly large class, so we will view it in sections. Open up the DungeonManager for editing. You can see the first section of DungeonManager in *Code Snip 4.1*:

```
1 using UnityEngine;
2 using System;
3 using System.Collections.Generic;
4 using Random = UnityEngine.Random;
```

```
5
6 public enum TileType {
7   essential, random, empty
8 }
9
10 public class DungeonManager : MonoBehaviour {
```

We are going to need a list, a dictionary, and some PRNs for our `Dungeon` class. `Lines 2-4` will enable these things for our use. `Lines 6-8` introduces a global enumeration that we will use to keep track of our path types. Then, `Line 10` leads us into the `DungeonManager` definition, starting with a helper class called `PathTile` that can be seen in *Code Snip 4.2*.

 Enumerations are a great way to keep track of states. Our `PathTile` class can take on a few different states (essential and random) and can possibly take on more states in the future. Given the nature that a `PathTile` class can only be one state at a time, enumerations work like a state ID. The enumeration is really just a number relation, such as `essential = 1` and `random = 2`. The enumeration is more descriptive though, so if we had 100 states we could assign names to the states rather than having to look up each state's ID number. For more information on enumerations, check out `https://unity3d.com/learn/tutorials/modules/beginner/scripting/enumerations`.

```
11 [Serializable]
12 public class PathTile {
13   public TileType type;
14   public Vector2 position;
15   public List<Vector2> adjacentPathTiles;
16
17   public PathTile (TileType t, Vector2 p, int min, int max,
    Dictionary<Vector2, TileType> currentTiles) {
18     type = t;
19     position = p;
20    adjacentPathTiles = getAdjacentPath(min, max, currentTiles);
21   }
22
23   public List<Vector2> getAdjacentPath(int minBound, int
    maxBound, Dictionary<Vector2, TileType> currentTiles) {
24     List<Vector2> pathTiles = new List<Vector2> ();
25     if (position.y + 1 < maxBound &&
       !currentTiles.ContainsKey(new Vector2(position.x,
       position.y + 1))) {
```

```
26        pathTiles.Add(new Vector2(position.x, position.y + 1));
27      }
28      if (position.x + 1 < maxBound &&
        !currentTiles.ContainsKey(new Vector2(position.x + 1,
        position.y))) {
29        pathTiles.Add(new Vector2(position.x + 1, position.y));
30      }
31      if (position.y - 1 > minBound &&
        !currentTiles.ContainsKey(new Vector2(position.x,
        position.y - 1))) {
32        pathTiles.Add(new Vector2(position.x, position.y - 1));
33      }
34      if (position.x - 1 >= minBound &&
        !currentTiles.ContainsKey(new Vector2(position.x - 1,
        position.y)) && type != TileType.essential) {
35        pathTiles.Add(new Vector2(position.x - 1, position.y));
36      }
37      return pathTiles;
38    }
39 }
```

The `PathTile` class is going to make the rest of the `DungeonManager` implementation much easier. Each `PathTile` will calculate and keep track of the tiles that are adjacent to that tile. They will also hold their own position and their type, which could be E for essential or R for random. Let's take a closer look at the `PathTile` class in *Code Snip 4.2*:

- `Line 13`: type will hold a `TileType` enum value, which will refer to the type of tile as `TileType.essential`, `TileType.random`, or `TileType.empty`.

- `Line 14`: This is the position of the tile as `Vector2`.

- `Line 15`: `adjacentPathTiles` is the list that we will use to store the tiles next to the current `PathTile`.

- `Lines 17-21`: This is the `PathTile` constructor. We will call this to make a new PathTile.

- `Line 23`: `getAdjacentPath` is the function that will calculate which tiles are adjacent to this tile based on the Dungeon Board dimensions and current tiles that have been laid out. We call `getAdjacentPath` in the constructor of the `PathTile` class and it requires the minimum and maximum bound of the grid, as well as the current tile list of all the tiles current laid.

`GetAdjacentPath` uses four `if` statements to check adjacent tiles to the top, right, bottom, and left of the current `PathTile`. The conditional statements are based on whether the adjacent tile is within the grid dimensions and if the tile is already part of the dungeon tile list. The last `if` condition on `Line 31` checks the type for `TileType.essential` because we don't want essential `PathTiles` to move left (backwards), we want to force them right (forwards).

So, that is our helper class that is going to make the rest of the `DungeonManager` class simpler to implement. We are ready to develop the rest of the `DungeonManager` definition. *Code Snip 4.3* continues the `DungeonManager` class:

```
40  public Dictionary<Vector2, TileType> gridPositions = new
    Dictionary<Vector2, TileType> ();
41
42   public int minBound = 0, maxBound;
43
44   public static Vector2 startPos;
45
46   public Vector2 endPos;
47
48   public void StartDungeon () {
49     gridPositions.Clear ();
50     maxBound = Random.Range (50, 101);
51
52     BuildEssentialPath ();
53
54     BuildRandomPath ();
55   }
```

*Code Snip 4.3* shows the setup of the dungeon in the `DungeonManager` class. We declare all our variables in the first few lines, then use a driver function to generate separate parts of the dungeon. Let's take a look at the specifics from *Code Snip 4.3*:

- `Line 40`: `gridPositions` is the dictionary we are using to store the structure of the generated dungeon. This dictionary is similar to the one we used in the `BoardManager` class except our value is now `TileType`.

- `Line 42`: `minBound` and `maxBound` are the dimensions of our board grid. `minBound` is always `0`, but we set it up as a variable just in case we decide to change it later. `maxBound` is not initialized here because it will be randomly initialized later.

- Line 44: startPos is the entrance position of our dungeon. We are making it public static because it needs to be accessed by the Player class. The Player class will use the position data to move the player character to startPos, while the world board is being changed out for the dungeon board.

- Lines 48-55: StartDungeon is our driver function for our dungeon generator. In the function, we clear our dictionary because we will use the generator multiple times in a game. We then randomly choose the dimensions of the board grid. Our grid is a square so we only need to choose one number and it will represent the length of all four sides. A dungeon larger than 200 by 200 starts to add a significant amount of load time mostly due to the fact that we are generating so many outer wall tiles. Lastly, we call the functions that will build the dungeon's essential and random paths.

Now, we need to develop the logic behind building the actual dungeon. The first function involved is BuildEssentialPath. Within this function, we are going to use a little bit of randomness and a little bit of direction to create a path that spans our grid from left to right. The left-most point will be our entrance and the right most point will be our exit. *Code Snip 4.4* shows the function:

```
56 private void BuildEssentialPath () {
57   int randomY = Random.Range (0, maxBound + 1);
58   PathTile ePath = new PathTile (TileType.essential, new Vector2
     (0, randomY), minBound, maxBound, gridPositions);
59   startPos = ePath.position;
60
61   int boundTracker = 0;
62
63   while (boundTracker < maxBound) {
64     gridPositions.Add (ePath.position, TileType.empty);
65     int adjacentTileCount = ePath.adjacentPathTiles.Count;
66     int randomIndex = Random.Range (0, adjacentTileCount);
67     Vector2 nextEPathPos;
68     if (adjacentTileCount > 0) {
69       nextEPathPos = ePath.adjacentPathTiles [randomIndex];
70     } else {
71       break;
72     }
73   PathTile nextEPath = new PathTile (TileType.essential,
     nextEPathPos, minBound, maxBound, gridPositions);
74     if (nextEPath.position.x > ePath.position.x ||
       (nextEPath.position.x == maxBound - 1 &&
       Random.Range (0,2) == 1)) {
75       ++boundTracker;
```

```
76      }
77      ePath = nextEPath;
78    }
79
80    if (!gridPositions.ContainsKey (ePath.position))
81      gridPositions.Add (ePath.position, TileType.empty);
82
83    endPos = new Vector2 (ePath.position.x, ePath.position.y);
84  }
```

BuildEssentialPath is going to run a loop that can potentially loop through every space in our grid. It is unlikely this will happen but we need to be aware of it. This means that in a worst-case scenario, a 100 x 100 dungeon can cause a loop to process 10,000 spaces, which is why any dungeon over 200 x 200 begins to load significantly more slowly. An important part of algorithm design is understanding what can happen in the worst case to gauge an average speed of execution.

It is very unlikely that we will see this worst case because our dungeon can take so many other forms. So let's take a look at the first step of our dungeon generator. We will go through *Code Snip 4.4* to see how we generate an essential path:

- Line 57: Here, we choose a random *y* coordinate for our entrance. We will always start our entrance on the extreme left, which is minBound. In this case, minBound is always 0.
- Line 58: ePath is a container for our current PathTile. We will store the current essential PathTile here and add it to our Dungeon Board after we decide which adjacent tile to follow. Initially, we will set it to our entrance location.
- Line 59: We need to set startPos to the entrance position so we can inform the Player class where to move the player character.
- Line 61: We will use a local integer variable to track how far along the grid length we are. Every time the essential path moves right, we will add 1 to boundTracker till boundTracker equals maxBound.
- Lines 63-84: This while loop will loop through tile spaces in our grid. It will end when our essential path has reached the right side of our grid.
- Line 64: The first thing we do is add the current PathTile to our dictionary. Remember, the first PathTile is the entrance.
- Line 65: Here, we find out how many tiles are adjacent to the current tile.
- Line 66: From the adjacent tile, we randomly choose one to follow.

- Lines `68-72`: This is our first check. We need to make sure that there are adjacent tiles before we continue. If there are no adjacent tiles and we reference an empty index, we will cause an error. However, we can assume that if there are no adjacent tiles, then we have hit the end of the grid and can break the loop early.

- Line `73`: If there are adjacent tiles, we store them as the next essential `PathTile`.

- Lines `74-76`: This check will determine whether or not the essential path has moved right. If it has, then we need to update the `boundTracker` to reflect that.

- Line `77`: At this point, we have made all the checks we need to use the current essential `PathTile` and the adjacent essential `PathTile`. We can set the adjacent tile to the current so that in the next iteration of the loop, it will be added to the list the process repeats.

- Lines `78-83`: Finally, once the loop has completed all its iterations, we add a check to see if the final essential `PathTile` was added to the dungeon dictionary. Remember that the loop could have broken early so we may have not added that last tile. Then, we set the last tile to the exit position, `endPos`.

So, just like in our algorithm design, our essential path builds out one tile at a time as it follows a random path that can only move in the directions up, down, and right. The essential path should be fairly winding, but it will be narrow as well. What's more, the path only moves in one direction, which is not very interesting. So we will introduce some random branches from the essential path.

The `BuildRandomPath` function, which is called just after the `BuildEssentialPath` function, will add onto the essential path in two ways. First, it will go through the essential `PathTiles` and see if there is an open adjacent tile that can branch off into an alternate path. Then, it might choose to build an opening called a chamber at the end of that path. *Code Snip 4.5* shows the implementation of `BuildRandomPath`:

```
85 private void BuildRandomPath () {
86   List<PathTile> pathQueue = new List<PathTile> ();
87   foreach (KeyValuePair<Vector2,TileType> tile in gridPositions)
     {
88     Vector2 tilePos = new Vector2(tile.Key.x, tile.Key.y);
89     pathQueue.Add(new PathTile(TileType.random, tilePos,
       minBound, maxBound, gridPositions));
90   }
91
92   pathQueue.ForEach (delegate (PathTile tile) {
93
94     int adjacentTileCount = tile.adjacentPathTiles.Count;
```

```
95      if (adjacentTileCount != 0) {
96        if (Random.Range(0, 5) == 1) {
97          BuildRandomChamber (tile);
98        }
99        else if (Random.Range (0, 5) == 1 || (tile.type ==
          TileType.random && adjacentTileCount > 1)) {
100         int randomIndex = Random.Range (0, adjacentTileCount);
101
102         Vector2 newRPathPos =
            tile.adjacentPathTiles[randomIndex];
103
104         if (!gridPositions.ContainsKey(newRPathPos)) {
105           gridPositions.Add (newRPathPos, TileType.empty);
106
107           PathTile newRPath = new PathTile (TileType.random,
              newRPathPos, minBound, maxBound, gridPositions);
108           pathQueue.Add (newRPath);
109         }
110       }
111     }
112   });
113 }
```

BuildRandomPath will introduce the use of the queue we discussed in our algorithm design earlier in this chapter. This queue will be used to take a copy of the essential path so that we can iterate over it. As we iterate over the queue and process the items, we will add new random PathTiles to the end of the queue. Once the queue is empty, our dungeon is complete. So let's take a look at how BuildRandomPath works:

- Line 86: We are going to use a list as our queue because it is easy to add to the end and remove from the front of the list.

- Lines 87-89: Using a foreach loop, we copy the essential path to the pathQueue.

- Lines 92-113: Now, we use a foreach loop on our queue and start processing PathTiles.

- Lines 94-95: We need to check if the current tile has any adjacent tiles.

- Lines 96-98: This check creates a 1 in 5 chance that the tile will become a chamber. We have a separate function that will build chambers.

- Line 99: Random paths generate randomly, meaning, there is a chance they won't generate at all. This check creates another 1 in 5 chance that a path will generate from an essential PathTile. However, if the current tile is a random PathTile and it has more than one direction to move, it will continue to develop. This just makes the random paths a little more wild.

- Lines `102-108`: If a random `PathTile` is to be placed, we check to make sure it isn't already part of the dungeon. We then add the new random `PathTile` to `gridPositions` and to the end of the queue. Eventually, the queue will come to this newly added `PathTile` and process it as well.

Eventually, probability or the size restriction of our grid will make it so that no new random `PathTiles` are added to the queue. Once the queue runs out of tiles to process the function terminates. We are left with a dictionary full of tile positions. But before that, we have to see how the `BuildRandomChamber` function works in *Code Snip 4.6*:

```
114 private void BuildRandomChamber (PathTile tile) {
115   int chamberSize = 3,
116     adjacentTileCount = tile.adjacentPathTiles.Count,
117     randomIndex = Random.Range (0, adjacentTileCount);
118   Vector2 chamberOrigin = tile.adjacentPathTiles[randomIndex];
119
120   for (int x = (int) chamberOrigin.x; x < chamberOrigin.x +
      chamberSize; x++) {
121     for (int y = (int) chamberOrigin.y; y < chamberOrigin.y +
        chamberSize; y++) {
122       Vector2 chamberTilePos = new Vector2 (x, y);
123       if (!gridPositions.ContainsKey(chamberTilePos) &&
          chamberTilePos.x < maxBound && chamberTilePos.x > 0 &&
          chamberTilePos.y < maxBound && chamberTilePos.y > 0)
124
125         gridPositions.Add (chamberTilePos, TileType.empty);
126     }
127   }
127 }
```

The `BuildRandomChamber` function is called in the `BuildRandomPath` function. This function is much like the type of PCG dungeon generation in which you connect some number of predefined level assets. In this case, we add a 3 x 3 chamber to the end of a random path. We could have made that 3 x 3 chamber a prefab, which would have been less code but more storage the game would need more storage. Instead, we generate it at runtime. Let's see how in *Code Snip 4.6*:

- Line `114-118`: We pass in the current `PathTile` that we are processing from the queue. We set the size of the chamber to 3 but this can easily be randomized. Next, we randomly choose an adjacent tile and set that as the origin of the chamber.

- Lines 120-130: Knowing the origin point and size of the chamber, we can loop through the tiles we need to add. This is very similar to the line of sight algorithm we used to reveal the world board in the previous chapter. At the end, we add the new tiles to the dictionary.

At this point, all of our dungeon coordinates have been generated and stored. We need to actually lay the floor and wall tiles now so that the player can see the dungeon onscreen and interact with it. We are going to use the BoardManager class for this.

# BoardManager

The BoardManager class already keeps references to the floor and wall tiles. Rather than having our DungeonManager class keep the same references, we will send our dungeon dictionary to the BoardManager class and have it build the Dungeon Board. We will need to update our BoardManager class for this. Open up BoardManager.cs for editing and make the changes seen in *Code Snip 4.7*:

```
29 public GameObject exit;
...
33 public GameObject[] outerWallTiles;
...
40 private Transform dungeonBoardHolder;
41 private Dictionary<Vector2, Vector2> dungeonGridPositions;
...
69 private void addTiles(Vector2 tileToAdd) {
70    if (!gridPositions.ContainsKey (tileToAdd)) {
71       gridPositions.Add (tileToAdd, tileToAdd);
72       GameObject toInstantiate = floorTiles [Random.Range (0,
          floorTiles.Length)];
73       GameObject instance = Instantiate (toInstantiate, new
          Vector3 (tileToAdd.x, tileToAdd.y, 0f),
          Quaternion.identity) as GameObject;
74       instance.transform.SetParent (boardHolder);
75
76       if (Random.Range (0, 3) == 1) {
77          toInstantiate = wallTiles [Random.Range
             (0,wallTiles.Length)];
78          instance = Instantiate (toInstantiate, new Vector3
             (tileToAdd.x, tileToAdd.y, 0f), Quaternion.identity) as
             GameObject;
79          instance.transform.SetParent (boardHolder);
80       }
81
82       if (Random.Range (0, 100) == 1) {
```

```
83        toInstantiate = exit;
84        instance = Instantiate (toInstantiate, new Vector3
          (tileToAdd.x, tileToAdd.y, 0f), Quaternion.identity) as
          GameObject;
85        instance.transform.SetParent (boardHolder);
86      }
87    }
88  }
...
141 public void SetDungeonBoard (Dictionary<Vector2,TileType>
    dungeonTiles, int bound, Vector2 endPos) {
142    boardHolder.gameObject.SetActive (false);
143    dungeonBoardHolder = new GameObject ("Dungeon").transform;
144    GameObject toInstantiate, instance;
145
146    foreach(KeyValuePair<Vector2,TileType> tile in
       dungeonTiles) {
147      toInstantiate = floorTiles [Random.Range (0,
         floorTiles.Length)];
148      instance = Instantiate (toInstantiate, new Vector3
         (tile.Key.x, tile.Key.y, 0f), Quaternion.identity) as
         GameObject;
149      instance.transform.SetParent (dungeonBoardHolder);
150    }
151
152    for (int x = -1; x < bound + 1; x++) {
153      for (int y = -1; y < bound + 1; y++) {
154        if (!dungeonTiles.ContainsKey(new Vector2(x, y))) {
155          toInstantiate = outerWallTiels [Random.Range (0,
             outerWallTiles.Length)];
156          instance = Instantiate (toInstantiate, new Vector3
             (x, y, 0f), Quaternion.identity) as GameObject;
157          instance.transform.SetParent (dungeonBoardHolder);
158        }
159      }
160    }
161
162    toInstantiate = exit;
163    instance = Instantiate (toInstantiate, new Vector3
       (endPos.x, endPos.y, 0f), Quaternion.identity) as
       GameObject;
164    instance.transform.SetParent (dungeonBoardHolder);
165  }
166
167 public void SetWorldBoard () {
```

```
168     Destroy (dungeonBoardHolder.gameObject);
169     boardHolder.gameObject.SetActive (true);
170 }
```

Keep in mind that the printed line number of *Code Snip 4.7* might not match perfectly with the code in your `BoardManager.cs` file. They should be close though. We will go over the relative position of the code in *Code Snip 4.7* as part of the following explanation:

- `Line 29`: `exit` is the the exit tile sprite that we are using as our dungeon entrance and exit marker. This should be placed near the other tile references.

- `Line 33`: `outerWallTiles` are the impassable wall tiles we will use to enclose our dungeon. This line should be placed somewhere near the other tile references.

- `Line 40-41`: We are going to use a separate transform and dictionary for the dungeon. This will prevent any cross over between the world board and the Dungeon Board as they will exist in the same scene. These lines should be placed near the world board transform and dictionary.

- `Lines 69-88`: The `addTiles` function was already declared, but we will be adding `Lines 82-86`.

- `Lines 82-86`: This small addition creates a probability that for every 1 in 100 tiles that are revealed on the world board, there will be an exit tile spawned. This exit tile would then act as an entrance to a randomly generated dungeon. You can change how frequently the exit tiles spawn by changing the `Random.Range`.

- `Lines 141-165`: The function `SetDungeonBoard` is a new addition to our `BoardManager` class. This function will take the dungeon data and apply the on screen graphics.

- `Line 142`: Instead of changing the scene, we will set the world board as inactive so that it is removed from the screen. Then, our Dungeon Board will be active and shown instead.

- `Line 143-149`: The dungeon coordinates are passed in as an argument. We can use a `foreach` loop to iterate over them and place the corresponding sprites.

- `Lines 152-160`: This nested `for` loop will traverse the perimeter of the dungeon and place a layer of outer wall tiles to enclose the dungeon. We will also fill in the empty space of the grid in this nested `for` loop with more outer wall tiles.

- `Lines 162-164`: Lastly, for the `SetDungeonBoard` function, we place the exit tiles on the `endPos` of our dungeon data.

- Lines 167-170: After exiting a dungeon, we want to reactivate the world board. We do that in these lines while destroying the old Dungeon Board so that it doesn't continue to take up space on our system.

So with these few updates to the BoardManager class, we were able to build and show an entered dungeon, set an entrance to the dungeon from the world board, and reactivate the world board by exiting the Dungeon Board. The Player class is going to need some updates as well. We are now placing an exit tile that will have a specific interaction with the player.

# Player

The Player class has to interact with the exit tile, which represents the entrance and exit of our dungeons. The player character also has to be transported to the Dungeon Board when the player moves to an exit tile. There are some subtleties to this, since we are not actually changing the scene. *Code Snip 4.8* shows the updates the Player class requires:

```
14 public bool onWorldBoard;
15 public bool dungeonTransition;
...
19 protected override void Start () {
20   animator = GetComponent<Animator>();
21
22   health = GameManager.instance.healthPoints;
23
24   healthText.text = "Health: " + health;
25
26   position.x = position.y = 2;27
27
28   onWorldBoard = true;
29   dungeonTransition = false;
30
31   base.Start ();
32 }
...
40 private void Update ()
...
63     if(horizontal != 0 || vertical != 0) {
64     if (!dungeonTransition) {
65     canMove = AttemptMove<Wall> (horizontal, vertical);
66     if(canMove && onWorldBoard) {
67     position.x += horizontal;
```

```
68      position.y += vertical;
69      GameManager.instance.updateBoard(horizontal, vertical);
70      }
71        }
72      }
...
137 private void GoDungeonPortal () {
138  if (onWorldBoard) {
139    onWorldBoard = false;
140    GameManager.instance.enterDungeon();
141    transform.position = DungeonManager.startPos;
142  } else {
143    onWorldBoard = true;
144    GameManager.instance.exitDungeon();
145    transform.position = position;
146  }
147 }
148
149 private void OnTriggerEnter2D (Collider2D other) {
150   if (other.tag == "Exit") {
151     dungeonTransition = true;
152     Invoke("GoDungeonPortal", 0.5f);
153     Destroy (other.gameObject);
154   }
155 }
```

Let's see how the changes connect with our dungeon generator:

- Lines 14-15: We are adding a couple of Boolean variables because we will need to switch some things on and off. onWorldBoard will let us know if we are on the world board, which will determine whether we track our position or not. dungeonTransition will let us know if we need to switch off our movement for a second, so we can transition to the dungeon entrance.

- Lines 28-29: Inside the Start function, we will initialize our new Boolean variables. We set onWorldBoard to true because we start on the world board. We set dungeonTransition to false because we don't initially begin transitioning to a dungeon.

- Line 64: We need to add a condition that when we are in transition to a dungeon entrance, we need to turn off movement. If we don't disable movement, then the player might try to continue to input movement. If half a movement is registered during the transition to a dungeon, it will cause some unusual behavior as the movement algorithm is now operating on an unintentional offset.

- Line 65: onWolrdBoard gets added to the movement conditional. Both the world board and Dungeon Board will exist simultaneously. If we don't turn off the player position tracking, we will reveal sections of the world board while in the dungeon.

- Lines 137-147: GoDungeonPortal is a two way function that manages the effect of the player interacting with the exit Tile. If the player is on the world board, then they enter a dungeon. If the player is in a dungeon, then they are sent back to the world board. Because we stop tracking player movement in a dungeon, we can send the player back to the world board position at which we transitioned to the dungeon.

- Lines 149-155: This is an override of a Unity built-in function. The exit tile has a Box Collider 2D that acts as a trigger. The OnTriggerEnter2D function will check if we hit an exit tile and begin the transition to the dungeon. We need to use Invoke to create a delay in the transition to match our movement delay. We then destroy the exit tile so we can't reactivate it.

At this point, the DungeonManager, BoardManager, and Player classes are all ready to interact with one another. We need to create a connection point for the information to be transferred between the classes. We will use the GameManager class for this task.

# GameManager

There are some small updates that we need to add to the GameManager class so that we can connect the Dungeon Board data to the BoardManager and Player classes. The GameManager class will use some driver functions to pass information to and from the different classes and initiate the dungeon generation. The update is shown in *Code Snip 4.9*:

```
16 private DungeonManager dungeonScript;
17 private Player playerScript;
...
22 void Awake() {
23   if (instance == null)
24     instance = this;
25   else if (instance != this)
26     Destroy(gameObject);
27
28   DontDestroyOnLoad(gameObject);
29
30   enemies = new List<Enemy>();
31
32   boardScript = GetComponent<BoardManager> ();
```

```
33
34   dungeonScript = GetComponent<DungeonManager> ();
35   playerScript = GameObject.FindGameObjectWithTag
     ("Player").GetComponent<Player> ();
36
37   InitGame();
38 }
...
116 public void enterDungeon () {
117    dungeonScript.StartDungeon ();
118    boardScript.SetDungeonBoard (dungeonScript.gridPositions,
       dungeonScript.maxBound, dungeonScript.endPos);
119    playerScript.dungeonTransition = false;
120 }
121
122 public void exitDungeon () {
123    boardScript.SetWorldBoard ();
124    playerScript.dungeonTransition = false;
125 }
```

These updates allow for some communication between the `Player`, `DungeonManager`, and `BoardManager` classes. Let's see how:

- `Lines 16-17`: We should add a reference to the `Player` and `DungeonManager` classes, so that we can exchange information and communication between them.

- `Lines 34-35`: Inside the `Awake` function, we initialize the `boardScript` and `playerScript` variables.

- `Lines 116-120`: The `enterDungeon` function drives the dungeon generation process. We call the function to generate the dungeon data then pass it to the `BoardManager` class to place the dungeon onscreen. We have to notify the `Player` class that the dungeon transition has occurred.

- `Lines 122-125`: The `enterDungeon` function drives the return to the world board. It calls the `SetWorldBoard` function from the `BoardManager` class and informs the `Player` class that the transition is over.

This completes all the code updates needed to fully implement our dungeon generator feature. It is almost time to see our creation in action. However, there are now some new parts that need our attention back in the Unity Editor.

# Back to the Unity Editor

In the **GameManager** prefab, we now have an array section for outer wall tiles. We will first need to set this up to reference the three different outer wall tiles that should already be in your **Prefabs** folder. You can add them by following these steps:

1. Select the **GameManager** prefab in the **Prefabs** folder.

2. Select the **Size** field under the **Outer Wall Tiles** section of the **Board Manager** component, set it to 3 and press *Enter*.

3. Drag and drop the outer wall tiles to the newly created outer wall tiles element fields.

We then need to add the DungeonManager script to the GameManager prefab. You can do that by following these steps:

1. Select the **GameManager** prefab in the **Prefabs** folder.

2. Click on the **Add Component** button under **Scripts | DungeonManager.cs**.

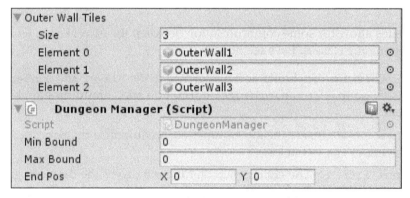

New options in the GameManager prefab

You have just completed the dungeon generator feature implementation. You can press the play button and give it a try. Once you have found a dungeon and entered it, you can press the pause button and view the entire dungeon in the **Scene** viewport.

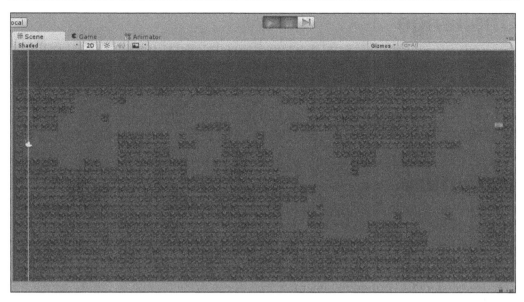

Image of dungeon overview

There is one last thing to discuss before the chapter is officially closed. Currently, we enter a dungeon and then destroy that dungeon upon exiting. We do this to save space, but it means our dungeon is gone and it would be unlikely that our dungeon generator will ever make the same dungeon twice. This is where seeds come in.

# Seeding the dungeon

We can set a seed value for any dungeon to recreate that dungeon. There is a simple way to test this as well. In the `DungeonManager.cs` file, add the line `Random.seed = 1;` to the top of the definition of the `StartDungeon` function.

Now return to the Unity Editor and play the game. Enter a dungeon and take a screenshot of the overview. Then, end the game and play again. Enter a dungeon and compare its overview to that of the screenshot. You will see that they have the exact same shape.

This is how we can destroy an entire randomly generated dungeon, yet return to it at a later time. You can adapt this line of code for situations such as having a player return to a dungeon to complete a task. For now, you can comment this line out because we won't be using it for our game, but feel free to experiment.

# Challenge

Recall our `BuildEssentialPath` function. If you decided to research the A* path-finding algorithm, you might have noticed that the `BuildEssentialPath` function is close to A*. As a challenge, you should replace our path-finding algorithm with an A* variant, as it will be far more efficient. Also, if you trim the outer wall tiles to only surround the path of the dungeon, you will decrease the load time and be able to make larger dungeons faster.

# Summary

Our *Roguelike* game is developing into an ever more interesting adventure. With the addition of our PCG dungeon generator, we are ready to do some dungeon crawling. There was quite a bit that we went over in this chapter, so let's summarize what we covered.

You designed a PCG dungeon generator that doesn't rely on player input like the world board. You learned how to effectively utilize a queue to process our Dungeon Board data. You developed a dungeon generator capable of utilizing both random paths and larger level asset placement. Finally, you got to see firsthand how to recreate a previously generated dungeon by seeding the PRN generator.

This concludes our level generation portion of the game. You have all you need to expand and adapt the code for a truly expansive and uniquely interesting game world. Take some time to experiment with the world board and Dungeon Board to see what you come up with. Now, our player needs some items and weapons to prepare himself for the coming enemies.

We are going to look at placing items in our world. Of course, these items will be random in nature, but they will play a role in how difficult the game becomes later on. We have a lot going on in our game world as well, so we need to be a little more precise in how we deliver items to the player; all of this and more in the next chapter.

# 5
# Randomized Items

Items in a game usually make up a considerable amount of content, especially in games where collecting loot is the main objective. We can use PCG to help us vary our content so that we don't have to create an overly large library of art assets. It is common in games that have a lot of content to use the same 3D model or sprite for two different items and just change the color or texture.

In this chapter, we are going to add items that our player can use to give them an advantage in the game. We will be adding both health items and items that can be stored in the player's inventory that will give the player bonus effects, such as damage and defense. We will randomize the values and use different colors to represent the strength of the item. This way, we can use the same sprite to represent several different item types. Here is a quick overview of what you will learn in this chapter:

- Designing a method to deliver items to the player
- Designing a method to randomly place items within the world and Dungeon Boards
- Using guided PRNs to determine the item's strength
- Learning to manipulate the color of a sprite so that it can be reused as several different items
- Creating a simple inventory

Content like items do need some sort of basis. This is usually a 3D model without a texture or a sprite drawn in gray-scale. We can then add the texture or color programmatically. It is possible to create sprites and 3D models programmatically as well, but this is very difficult if the model or sprite is complex or needs to be animated. Also, the 3D model or sprite might never quite match your game theme in the way a human designed art asset could.

With this caveat in mind, we will be doing a little art asset creation in this chapter. Another sprite sheet will be provided in the exercise files in the `Chapter 5` folder. However, feel free to create your own art base for color manipulation. We will go over the import method needed to get our new art assets in our game.

# Generating health items in the game world

Eventually, our player will be fighting for survival against an onslaught of baddies. It is inevitable that the player will take some health damage, so we need to provide a way for him or her to recover and continue playing. Providing the player with health recovery items is the most common approach. So, we will do just that but as usual we want to procedurally generate the items.

Rather than just randomly laying our health item tiles about the world board, we can use the environment we have created to add a layer of interactivity. The wall tiles that inhabit the world board are already laid at random. They are also destructible. We can, thus, use the wall tiles as a potential container for our health items.

By doing this, we have added a layer of game play for the player. The player now has to *forage* for their health items while confronted by foes. This should add to the suspense, difficulty, and reward factors, which contribute to the overall fun of the game.

## Implementing health item generation

With our first feature, health item generation, we have three tasks ahead of us:

- Modifying the `Wall` script
- Setting up sprites
- Interacting with health items

The first thing we have to do is modify our `Wall` script for the added functionality. The `Wall` script was written with the intention that the player would be able to destroy wall tiles. All we have to do is add a condition to the destruction of the wall that will spawn a food item. Food items will be our health items in this game. Open up `Wall.cs` for editing and take a look at the changes made to it in *Code Snip 5.1*:

```
1 using UnityEngine;
2 using System.Collections;
```

```
 3 using Random = UnityEngine.Random;
 4
 5 public class Wall : MonoBehaviour {
 6   public Sprite dmgSprite;
 7   public int hp = 3;
 8   public GameObject[] foodTiles;
 9
10   private SpriteRenderer spriteRenderer;
11
12   void Awake () {
13     spriteRenderer = GetComponent<SpriteRenderer> ();
14   }
15
16   public void DamageWall (int loss) {
17
18     spriteRenderer.sprite = dmgSprite;
19     hp -= loss;
20
21     if (hp <= 0) {
22       if (Random.Range (0,5) == 1) {
23         GameObject toInstantiate = foodTiles [Random.Range (0,
           foodTiles.Length)];
24         GameObject instance = Instantiate (toInstantiate, new
           Vector3 (transform.position.x, transform.position.y,
           0f), Quaternion.identity) as GameObject;
25         instance.transform.SetParent (transform.parent);
26       }
27
28       gameObject.SetActive (false);
29     }
30   }
31 }
```

*Code Snip 5.1* shows `Wall.cs` with the necessary changes. Let's see what was done:

- `Line 3`: We set `Random` to be the `UnityEngine.Random` library as we have done before. Remember that there are two random libraries, one is the C# language built-in and the other is the Unity built-in.

- `Line 8`: We are going to add a `GameObject` array to hold the two different food item tiles. We use the same technique in our `BoardManager` class with the other tile types.

- Lines 22-26: This is the wall destruction condition. Given a certain probability dictated by a PRN value, we set a food tile in place of the wall tile. The actual instantiation of the food tile is the same technique we use in the BoardManager class.

This is a fairly quick and easy adjustment to the Wall class to make it yield food items. At this point, we are potentially creating a paradigm by making destructible objects that will produce items for the player. It might be a good idea to make a base class that controls the general functionality of the Wall class and any class like the wall. This was done for the Player class inheriting the MovingObject class because we anticipate a similar Enemy class. This base class creation will be left up to you, though.

## Setting up sprites

In order to have our food items appear on screen, we need to set up their sprites. Go back to the Unity Editor. We are going to make two more prefabs represent the food items:

1. From the top menu, navigate to **GameObject | Create Empty**.
2. Select the new empty object in the **Hierarchy** panel.
3. Name the object Food.
4. Set **Layer** to **Items**.
5. Add the tag **Food**.
6. Click on the **Add Component** button in the **Inspector** tab and add a **Sprite Renderer** and a **Box Collider 2D**.
7. In the **Sprite** field of the **Sprite Renderer** component, select **Scavangers_ SpriteSheet_19**.
8. In the **Sorting Layer** field of the **Sprite Renderer** component, set **Sorting Layer** to **Items**.

9. In the **Box Collider 2D** component, check the **Is Trigger** checkbox.

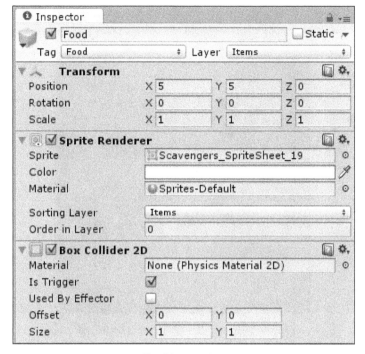

Food item setting

You can drag and drop the new **Food** prefab into the **Prefabs** folder and delete it from the **Hierarchy** panel. You are going to do the same thing for the second food prefab, which we will call `Soda`. However, for step 3, name the GameObject `Soda`, and set the tag to `Soda` as well. Use the **Scavangers_SpriteSheet_18** file in step 7 for your sprite.

We now have to add the food items to the **Wall** prefabs. Select all 8 **Wall** prefabs so that we can edit them at the same time. Under the **Food Tiles** array field, set the size to 2. Then, drag and drop the **Food** and **Soda** prefabs into the newly created element slots and delete the **Food** and **Soda** prefabs from the **Hierarchy** panel.

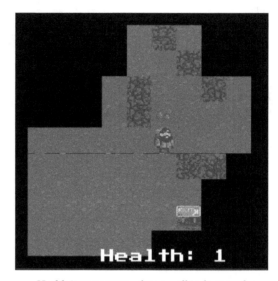

Health item appears when a wall is destroyed

If you play the game now, our health items should be active. Try destroying some wall tiles to produce some health items. You will notice that we can't actually interact with the items yet. We need to make another adjustment in our code that will allow the player to pick up the health item. This will be done in the Player.cs file, and *Code Snip 5.2* shows the changes:

```
134 private void UpdateHealth (Collider2D item) {
135  if (health < 100) {
136    if (item.tag == "Food") {
137      health += Random.Range (1,4);
138    } else {
139      health += Random.Range (4,11);
140    }
141    GameManager.instance.healthPoints = health;
142    healthText.text = "Health: " + health;
143  }
144 }
145 private void OnTriggerEnter2D (Collider2D other) {
146  if (other.tag == "Exit") {
147    dungeonTransition = true;
148    Invoke ("GoDungeonPortal", 0.5f);
```

```
149    Destroy (other.gameObject);
150  } else if (other.tag == "Food" || other.tag == "Soda") {
151    UpdateHealth(other);
152    Destroy (other.gameObject);
153  }
154 }
```

The changes needed in the `Player.cs` file come at the end of the file. We need a function that will update our player health, and then we need to update the `OnTriggerEnter2D` method so that we can interact with health items. Let's take a look at how the functions work:

- Lines `134-144`: `UpdateHealth` will update our health value that is displayed at the bottom of the screen in game play. It takes a `Collider2D` that we will pass in from the `OnTriggerEnter2D` function.

- Line `135`: We don't want to exceed our maximum health so we will need to make sure we are under 100.

- Line `136-140`: We check to see if the item is `Food` or `Soda`. We will say that `Soda` provides more health than `Food`. But in the PCG fashion, we will let PRNs dictate the specific value of health we gain from the health items.

- Line `141-142`: Here, we make adjustments to the health value that the player sees.

- Lines `145-154`: The `OnTriggerEnter2D` function was used in the previous chapter to make it possible for the player to enter a dungeon.

- Line `150-153`: We added another tag check to detect a collision with `Food` or `Soda`. If we hit a health item, we are going to call our newly added `UpdateHealth` function.

You can return to the Unity Editor to test the new health item functionality. First, you will want to set your health below 100. You can do this by selecting the **GameManager** prefab in the **Prefabs** folder and setting **Health Points** to some value less than 100.

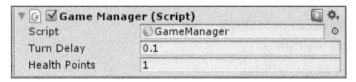

Where to find and set health points

Now, you can play the game. Destroy some walls to produce some health items. When you walk over the health item, you will see the health value onscreen increase. This will aid the player in surviving in the game. Adding health items was an almost easy task, but it gave us some insight on how we might approach our next item addition.

# Generating items in the dungeon

Usually in RPG games, the player will acquire and carry items that add some status boosting effects. The player can have weapons to increase their damage or armor to increase their defense. We are going to add some **armor** items that will power up our player.

The armor items will run on a slightly more complicated system than the health items and will require their own class. We will also need a way to deliver the items to the player. We want to be a little more interesting than just littering the dungeon floor with items, so we will create a chest that will randomly spawn items.

## The Chest prefab

Let's start with the Chest prefab. The Chest prefab will be a lot like the Wall prefab, in that the Chest prefab will also spawn items upon iteration. We will begin by building the prefab.

This chapter includes some additional art assets that can be imported for the Chest prefab and armor items. You are welcome to take this opportunity to make your own art for this part. You can find the provided sprite sheet in the exercise files in the Chapter 5 folder.

We will now go over the whole import process:

1. In **Projects**, select the **Sprites** folder.
2. Right-click either on the folder icon or anywhere in the folder.
3. From the right-click menu, select **Import New Asset...**.
4. Navigate to and select the Items_Sprite_Sheet.png file or your sprite sheet.

You now have a new unformatted sprite sheet available in the **Sprites** folder. We want to match the setting of the previous sprite sheet. Select the **Items_Sprite_Sheet. png** file so that we can view it's settings in the **Inspector** tab, and follow these steps:

1. Set **Sprite Mode** to **Multiple**.
2. Set **Pixels Per Unit** to 32.
3. Set **Filter Mode** to **Point**.

4. Set **Max Size** to **1024**.

5. Set **Format** to **Truecolor**.

6. Click on **Apply**.

Imported sprite sheet settings

Now, we need to set up the slicing of the image. While `Items_Sprite_Sheet.png` is still selected, find and click on the **Sprite Editor** button. Here, we can make sure that our sprites are properly sized.

For each sprite:

1. Select a sprite. You will notice a blue bounding box around the selected sprite.

2.  Set both, the width (**W**) and height (**H**) to 32. You might need to move the bounding box to accept a width and height of 32.

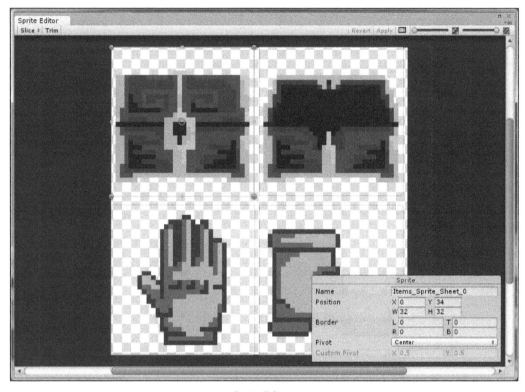

Sprite Editor

You can then click on **Apply** in the upper-right corner of the Sprite Editor. Exit the Sprite Editor. If the sprite sheet hasn't expanded in the **Sprites** folder, you can click on the white arrow on the side of the sprite to expand it. You can then inspect the individual sprites and make sure their dimensions are correct. Before we start coding, we are going to create the Chest prefab:

1.  From the top menu, navigate to **GameObject | Create Empty**.
2.  Select the new empty object in the **Hierarchy** panel.
3.  Name the object `Chest`.
4.  Set **Layer** to **BlockingLayer**.
5.  Click on the **Add Component** button in the **Inspector** tab and add **Sprite Renderer** and **Box Collider 2D** components.
6.  In the **Sprite** field of the **Sprite Renderer** component, select **Items_Sprite_ Sheet_0**.

7. In the **Sorting Layer** field of the **Sprite Renderer** component, set the **Sorting Layer** field to **Units**.

8. Drag and drop the new **Chest** prefab into the **Prefabs** folder and delete it from the **Hierarchy** panel.

# Chest implementation

We are ready to start coding the functionality of the chest. As stated previously in the chapter, the chest code is very similar to the wall code. It would be a better practice to make a base class that the chest and wall can inherit from but we are going to take the lazy route. You should challenge yourself to make this base class on your own.

We will be making a new class for the chest, so inside the **Scripts** folder, right-click and select **Create | C# Script** and name it Chest.cs. You can then open the Chest.cs script for editing. *Code Snip 5.3* shows the whole class definition:

```
1 using UnityEngine;
2 using System.Collections;
3
4 public class Chest : MonoBehaviour {
5
6   public Sprite openSprite;
7 // public Item randomItem;
8
9   private SpriteRenderer spriteRenderer;
10
11   void Awake () {
12     spriteRenderer = GetComponent<SpriteRenderer> ();
13   }
14
15   public void Open () {
16     spriteRenderer.sprite = openSprite;
17
18 //    randomItem.RandomItemInit ();
19 //    GameObject toInstantiate = randomItem.gameObject;
20 //    GameObject instance = Instantiate (toInstantiate, new
           Vector3 (transform.position.x, transform.position.y, 0f),
           Quaternion.identity) as GameObject;
21 //    instance.transform.SetParent (transform.parent);
22
23     gameObject.layer = 10;
24     spriteRenderer.sortingLayerName = "Items";
25   }
26 }
```

We are using a structure similar to the wall. We have already seen most of what is happening in the Chest class. Let's take a look at what we have done:

- Lines 4-26: This is the Chest class definition.

- Line 6: This is a reference to the sprite that will show that the chest has been opened.

- Line 7: This will be the randomized item that the chest spawns. It is commented out right now because we haven't made the Item class yet and this code will cause an error.

- Line 9: This is the reference to the **Sprite Renderer** component so that we can change the sprite when we need to.

- Lines 11-13: The Awake function will set the spriteRenderer variable to the chest's Sprite Renderer component.

- Lines 15-25: The Open function will switch the sprite and spawn the randomized item.

- Line 18: RandomItemInit will be the call we make to our Item class when we create it later in the chapter.

- Lines 18-21: These lines will be commented out till we make our Item class. If they are uncommented, they will cause an error.

- Line 23: Here, we set the layer to one farther down the list, so that we can walk over the opened chests.

- Line 24: Here, we set the sorting layer to a lower layer so that when we walk over the chest, it will appear under us.

Now, you can return to the Unity Editor and add the script to the **Chest** prefab. In the **Open Sprite** field, select **Items_Sprite_Sheet_1**. At this point, our **Chest** prefab is done except that there are no items for it to spawn. We also need to add the code that will spawn the chest.

## Spawning the chest

We are going to utilize our public enum TileType for the chest spawning. The TileType enumeration is in the DungeonManager.cs file. We are going to add chest to the enumeration set. TileType will look like the following *Code Snip 5.4*:

```
1 public enum TileType {
2   essential, random, empty, chest
3 }
...
143 if (Random.Range (0, 70) == 1) {
```

```
144    gridPositions.Add (chamberTilePos, TileType.chest);
145 } else {
146   gridPositions.Add (chamberTilePos, TileType.empty);
147 }
```

At the end of the `DungeonManager.cs` file, we also make an addition to the
`BuildRandomChamber` function. We see that change at the end of *Code Snip 5.4*. `Line`
`143` creates a probability that a chest will spawn on any given tile within a chamber
area of a dungeon. On `Line 144`, we then set `TileType` to `TileType.chest` for
future reference. Now, we need to switch files to `BoardManager.cs`.

We need to add the reference to the **Chest** prefab. You can add the reference variable,
`public GameObject chestTile`, near the other references to the different tiles.
Then, the last adjustment that we need to make is in the `SetDungeonBoard` function.
*Code Snip 5.5* shows that change:

```
130 public void SetDungeonBoard (Dictionary<Vector2,TileType>
    dungeonTiles, int bound, Vector2 endPos) {
131   boardHolder.gameObject.SetActive (false);
132   dungeonBoardHolder = new GameObject ("Dungeon").transform;
133   GameObject toInstantiate, instance;
134
135   foreach(KeyValuePair<Vector2,TileType> tile in dungeonTiles)
      {
136     toInstantiate = floorTiles [Random.Range (0,
        floorTiles.Length)];
137     instance = Instantiate (toInstantiate, new Vector3
        (tile.Key.x, tile.Key.y, 0f), Quaternion.identity) as
        GameObject;
138     instance.transform.SetParent (dungeonBoardHolder);
139
140     if (tile.Value == TileType.chest) {
141       toInstantiate = chestTile;
142       instance = Instantiate (toInstantiate, new Vector3
          (tile.Key.x, tile.Key.y, 0f), Quaternion.identity) as
          GameObject;
143       instance.transform.SetParent (dungeonBoardHolder);
144     }
145   }
...
```

The `SetDungeonBoard` function was written in *Chapter 4, Generating Random Dungeons*.
Now, we will add `Lines 140-144`. We use the tile value in our dictionary to check
whether the tile has a chest on it. If it does, then we instantiate the chest tile the same
way we have been instantiating everything.

At this point, we can return to the Unity Editor. Drag and drop the **Chest** prefab into the **Chest Tile** field of the **Board Manager** script in the **GameManager** prefab. If you play the game and enter a dungeon, you should eventually find a chest. If you do not find any, you can go back to the `DungeonManager.cs` file and adjust the probability at which they spawn.

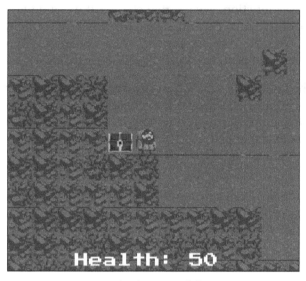

A randomly spawned chest

When you encounter a chest, nothing will happen. It will block you from moving but it won't open. We need to add the interaction functionality in the `Player` class, but it would be empty anyway.

We need some items for the chest to spawn. This is where our status modifying armor items come in. While we are in the Unity Editor, we can put together our Item prefab first.

# The Item prefab

The **Item** prefab will be similar to the **Food** prefab. We want the item to trigger on collision so that we can *pick up* the item. You can create the **Item** prefab as follows:

1. From the top menu, navigate to **GameObject** | **Create Empty**.

2. Select the new empty object in the **Hierarchy** panel.

3. Name the object `Item`.

4. Set **Tag** to **Item**.

5. Set **Layer** to **Items**.

6. Click on the **Add Component** button in the Inspector tab and add **Sprite Renderer** and **Box Collider 2D** components.

7. Leave the **Sprite** field of the **Sprite Renderer** component blank.

8. In the **Sorting Layer** field of the **Sprite Renderer** component, set the sorting layer to **Items**.

9. In the **Box Collider 2D** component, check the **Is Trigger** checkbox.

10. Drag and drop the new **Item** Prefab into the **Prefabs** folder and delete it from the **Hierarchy** panel.

# Item code

After the prefab is made, create a new script in the **Scripts** folder. You can name the script Item.cs. This will be our Item class. We are going to use one prefab and one script to morph the item into several different types of items. So, open up Item.cs for editing. The following *Code Snip 5.6* shows the full Item class:

```
1 using UnityEngine;
2 using System;
3 using Random = UnityEngine.Random;
4
5 public enum itemType {
6   glove, boot
7 }
8
9 public class Item : MonoBehaviour {
10
11   public Sprite glove;
12   public Sprite boot;
13
14   public itemType type;
15   public Color level;
16   public int attackMod, defenseMod;
17
18   private SpriteRenderer spriteRenderer;
19
20   public void RandomItemInit () {
21     spriteRenderer = GetComponent<SpriteRenderer> ();
22     SelectItem ();
23   }
24
```

```
25  private void SelectItem () {
26    var itemCount = Enum.GetValues(typeof(itemType)).Length;
27    type = (itemType)Random.Range(0,itemCount);
28
29    switch (type) {
30      case itemType.glove:
31        attackMod = Random.Range(1,4);
32        defenseMod = 0;
33        spriteRenderer.sprite = glove;
34        break;
35      case itemType.boot:
36        attackMod = 0;
37        defenseMod = Random.Range(1,4);
38        spriteRenderer.sprite = boot;
39        break;
40    }
41
42    int randomLevel = Random.Range(0, 100);
43    if (randomLevel >= 0 && randomLevel < 50) {
44      spriteRenderer.color = level = Color.blue;
45      attackMod += Random.Range(1,4);
46      defenseMod += Random.Range(1,4);
47    }
48    else if (randomLevel >= 50 && randomLevel < 75) {
49      spriteRenderer.color = level = Color.green;
50      attackMod += Random.Range(4,10);
51      defenseMod += Random.Range(4,10);
52    }
53    else if (randomLevel >= 75 && randomLevel < 90) {
54      spriteRenderer.color = level = Color.yellow;
55      attackMod += Random.Range(15,25);
56      defenseMod += Random.Range(15,25);
57    }
58    else {
59      spriteRenderer.color = level = Color.magenta;
60      attackMod += Random.Range(40,55);
61      defenseMod += Random.Range(40,55);
62    }
63  }
64 }
```

Let's take a look at how the Item class works:

- `Line 3`: Set `Random` to use `UnityEngine.Random`.

- `Lines 5-7`: We are making another public enumeration that will tell us the current kind of Item type, which is either a `glove` or `boot`.

- `Lines 11-12`: We will need a reference to the `glove` and `boot` sprites.

- `Line 14`: We will keep a variable that holds the items type for reference.

- `Line 15`: The color of the item is going to represent how powerful the item is.

- `Line 16`: The `attackMod` and `defenseMod` variables will be the actual numeric value that gets added to the player's attack power of defense.

- `Line 18`: We will need a reference to Sprite Renderer to change the sprite.

- `Lines 20-23`: This will be the function that is called by the `Chest` class when a chest is opened.

- `Lines 25-63`: The `SelectItem` function will generate the randomized Item.

- `Lines 26-27`: Randomly choose an Item type.

- `Lines 29-40`: Based on the type we input, the item will have a corresponding base value. The item will have a higher `attackMod` value if it is a glove or a higher `defenceMod` value if it is a boot.

- `Lines 42-62`: This section will change the color and adjust the modifiers. Blue is most likely to spawn but is the weakest. Magenta is the least likely to spawn and is the most powerful. The values are all randomized within a range so each item is a little different.

# Adding player to item interaction

Now, our randomized item class is ready to deploy. You can return to the Unity Editor and add the `Item` script to the **Item** prefab. There are some additional settings now that we will need to define:

- Set the sprite in the **Glove** field to **Items_Sprite_sheet_2**
- Set the sprite in the **Boot** field to **Items_Sprite_sheet_3**
- The other parameters are set at runtime by the script

We still need to implement the `Player` class interaction with the `Chest` and `Item` classes. Open up the `Player.cs` script for editing. *Code Snip 5.8* shows the changes needed for the item interaction:

```
16  public Image glove;
17  public Image boot;
18
19   public int attackMod = 0, defenseMod = 0;
20  private Dictionary<String, Item> inventory;
21
22  protected override void Start () {
23    animator = GetComponent<Animator>();
24    health = GameManager.instance.healthPoints;
25    healthText.text = "Health: " + health;
26    position.x = position.y = 2;
27    onWorldBoard = true;
28    dungeonTransition = false;
29
30    inventory = new Dictionary<String, Item> ();
31
32    base.Start ();
33      }
...
61 if(horizontal != 0 || vertical != 0) {
62  if (!dungeonTransition) {
63    if (onWorldBoard)
64      canMove = AttemptMove<Wall> (horizontal, vertical);
65    else
66      canMove = AttemptMove<Chest> (horizontal, vertical);
67
...
86  protected override void OnCantMove <T> (T component) {
87    if (typeof(T) == typeof(Wall)) {
88      Wall blockingObj = component as Wall;
89      blockingObj.DamageWall (wallDamage);
90    }
91    else if (typeof(T) == typeof(Chest)) {
92      Chest blockingObj = component as Chest;
93      blockingObj.Open ();
94    }
95
96    animator.SetTrigger ("playerChop");
97  }
...
```

```
146 private void UpdateInventory (Collider2D item) {
147   Item itemData = item.GetComponent<Item> ();
148   switch(itemData.type) {
149     case itemType.glove:
150       if (!inventory.ContainsKey("glove"))
151         inventory.Add("glove", itemData);
152       else
153         inventory["glove"] = itemData;
154
155       glove.color = itemData.level;
156     break;
157     case itemType.boot:
158       if (!inventory.ContainsKey("boot"))
159         inventory.Add("boot", itemData);
160       else
161         inventory["boot"] = itemData;
162
163       boot.color = itemData.level;
164     break;
165   }
166
167   attackMod = 0;
168   defenseMod = 0;
169
170   foreach (KeyValuePair<String, Item> gear in inventory) {
171     attackMod += gear.Value.attackMod;
172     defenseMod += gear.Value.defenseMod;
173   }
174 }
175
176 private void OnTriggerEnter2D (Collider2D other) {
177   if (other.tag == "Exit") {
178     dungeonTransition = true;
179     Invoke ("GoDungeonPortal", 0.5f);
180     Destroy (other.gameObject);
181   } else if (other.tag == "Food" || other.tag == "Soda") {
182     UpdateHealth(other);
183     Destroy (other.gameObject);
184   } else if (other.tag == "Item") {
185     UpdateInventory(other);
186     Destroy (other.gameObject);
187   }
188 }
```

We need to make changes throughout the `Player.cs` file. Luckily, they aren't too complicated or lengthy. Let's take a look at what was done:

- `Lines 16-17`: We are going to need to represent what items we have in our inventory. These references will be images on screen that show us the type of armor Items we are carrying.

- `Lines 19-20`: We add the modifiers for later use in the `Player` class. Items will now directly affect these player modifiers. We also add a dictionary that will be our inventory.

- `Line 30`: Inside the `Start` function, we initialize our inventory.

- `Lines 63-66`: Inside the `Update` function, we need to a check to see what blocking object we are sending to the `AttemptMove` function. For now, we assume that the player will only be blocked by walls on the world board and chests on the Dungeon Board.

- `Lines 86-97`: We made our `OnCantMove` function accept a generic type `T`, which will either be a wall or chest at the moment. So, we need to check the type of incoming blocking object. We then call that blocking object's public interaction method.

- `Lines 146-174`: The `UpdateInventory` method will be called when the player picks up a new Item. We are only going to allow one item of each type in our inventory at the moment, so we first check the Item type against what we currently have in our inventory. If we already have one item of that type, say boots, we replace it with the new boots we just picked up. Otherwise, we just accept the newly picked item into the empty slot in our inventory. We also want to change the color of our on screen inventory to match the color of the Item we just picked up. After, we calculate the new status modifier values.

- `Lines 176-188`: At the end of the `OnTriggerEnter2D` function, we add a check for the `Item` tag. We will call the `UpdateInventory` method from here if we run into an Item.

Before we return to the Unity Editor, we need to uncomment the commented code from our Chest.cs file. This will open up another field to edit in the **Chest** prefab. Once you uncomment the code, return to the Unity Editor and add the **Item** prefab to the **Random Item** field of the **Chest** prefab.

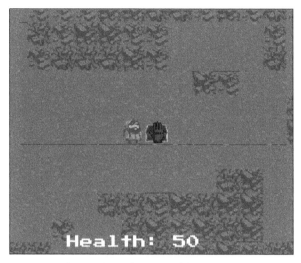

chest and item but no visible inventory

Now, we can play the game and see our item system in action. You can find a chest and open it to reveal a random item. However, you still can't pick it up. Even if you could pick up the item, you would really have no way of knowing what is in your inventory. We did write the code that would handle this though. We only need to add the UI elements that will display our inventory. Here is what we need to add:

1. In **Hierarchy**, right-click on the **Canvas** object.
2. Navigate to **UI** | **Image**.
3. Name image GloveImage.
4. Set both **Width** and Height to 50.
5. Set **Pos X** to -430 and **Pos Y** to -180.
6. Set **Source Image** to **Items_Sprite_Sheet_2**.
7. Create another image.
8. Name the image BootImage.
9. Set **Pos X** to -365 and **Pos Y** to -180.
10. Set **Source Image** to **Items_Sprite_Sheet_3**.

In order to activate the inventory images, we need to set the references in the **Player** prefab. Select the **Player** object in the **Hierarchy** panel and find the **Glove** and **Boot** fields in the **Inspector** tab. Drag and drop the **GloveImage** and **BootImage** respectively. Click on the **Apply** button at the top.

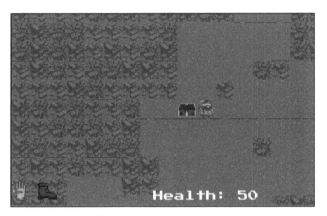

Picked up items show in inventory

Now, we have all we need to pick up items and actually see what we have in our inventory. Try this functionality out. While playing, view the player in the **Inspector** tab and look at the **Attack Mod** and **Defense Mod** fields. They will change with every item you pick up.

# Summary

For this chapter, we couldn't avoid adding in some art assets, but we were able to take those assets and multiply them. We figured out a good way to randomly place Items by implementing some health Items. Then, we expanded on that by spawning Chests that contain random armor Items. We only used two sprites for our armor Items but turned them into essentially eight different items.

You learned how to take some elements in our game environment and use them to our advantage, such as the wall tile yielding food items. You learned how to take a more subtle approach to randomly spawning assets into the game. We used highly guided PRNs to determine types of Items. You learned how to use something such as color to change the look of an item enough to make it a new item. And finally, we created a simple inventory base that can be expanded upon.

We are going to continue with the item theme in the next chapter. We have health items to heal us from enemy attacks and we have armor items to protect us from bad guys. All we need now is weapons to do some damage. The next chapter will introduce random modular weapons.

# 6
# Generating Modular Weapons

PCG is a great way to minimize the number of handcrafted art assets that we need to create for our game. However, it is unrealistic to think that we won't need any art assets at all. We can still use our art intelligently, and with the aid of PCG, a little art can go a long way.

In this chapter, we see how we can create small pieces of art that are combined in different ways to generate bigger and randomly unique assets. We will be creating a modular weapon system. Each piece of art is a module that will attach to another module to create a whole weapon. We can then let the pieces combine randomly to give us surprisingly unique assets.

Here is what you will learn in this chapter:

- Understanding modular art assets
- Learning about the statistics behind modular generation
- Procedurally generating game objects that are composed from smaller pieces
- Animating via a script

The weapons that will be generated from this modular weapon system will be used by our player character. Since we are generating an entirely unique asset from some existing assets, we will forfeit our use of sprite animation, which is derived from a sprite sheet. It isn't very interesting to just see the image of the weapon, though. We will also have to script some animation for the character in order for it to swing the weapon.

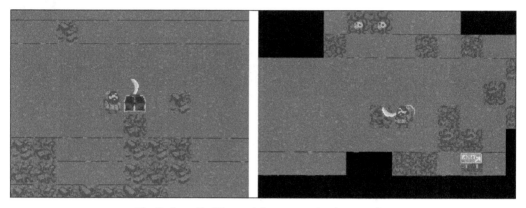

The final result of the modular weapon implementation

Once our weapon generation system is implemented, we will be able to easily add to it. The weapons will allow our player to attack and defend themselves. We are approaching the end of the development of our game, so let's jump in and keep the momentum going.

# PCG with modules

In software development, we strive to make our code modular. This means that we break our code down into smaller, simpler pieces, which are sometimes called modules. The point is to create larger systems out of pieces that can be reused in as many ways as possible. If we write code in this way, we can efficiently create similar systems and also increase our flexibility.

We could apply this concept to art, as well. If we separate a piece of art into its components, we can redraw each component in many different ways. Each component is a module, and we can swap modules to make a whole new piece of art.

An example of this would be a sword. A sword is made up of three basic components of modules, such as a blade, a hilt, and a handle. We can combine any blade with any hilt and handle, if we choose to. We will put this example into practice, as this will show exactly how we implement our modular weapons.

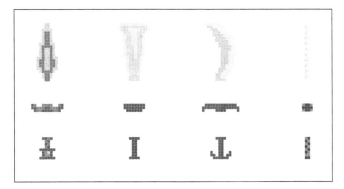

Weapon module sprites

# Statistics of modular PCG

Besides the fact that this system gives us randomly unique items in our game, there is another reason that this system is desirable. We can produce a small number of modular art assets and, in return, generate a large number of whole art assets. This, in turn, can save a lot of time and resources in our asset creation process.

We can give ourselves an idea of just how many items we can generate with a few modular pieces by doing a little math. Say, for example, we have four possible modules per component of the sword. This means that there are four blades, four hilts, and four handles, which comes up to 12 modules in total. The possible number of combinations of all these modules is as follows:

$$4*4*4 = 4^3 = 64$$

Comparing 12 modules to 64 whole art assets, we can see that we have just over five times the generated art assets than we do the modules. This is a pretty good return, but it doesn't end there. If we add just one more module to each type of component, with five blades, five hilts, and five handles, we now have this combination:

$$5*5*5 = 5^3 = 125$$

By adding only three more modules, we get over eight times the return in generated art assets. This is because we have created an exponential relation. Adding more modules will exponentially increase the number of ways in which they can be combined to generate whole art assets. This is extremely powerful as we can deliver our game with less baked-in information, making it smaller in size. Instead of creating 125 distinct art assets, we will have to only create 15 art assets. The variety that is a result of this method will keep our player interested for a longer period of time.

# Creating and configuring new sprites

It is beneficial to know exactly how the module sprite alignment works so that we can go a little more in-depth into the subject of sprite creation than in previous chapters. As stated in the preceding examples, we are going to create a sword as our modular weapon model. We will first need to add a new sprite sheet with our weapon modules. This particular sprite sheet will need some special considerations, though.

We will be overlaying the 2D sprites on top of one another. Each module will align in such a way that does not obstruct the view of the other modules. In order to do this with no mathematical calculation, we will create each module with a bounding box of the same size. This way, each sprite will occupy the same bounding space, but we will move the actual image to align with the other modules.

Note that this method of using identical bounding boxes is a simplification due to the animation that we will be adding. In a production grade video game, you would want to make the bounding boxes as small as possible, and use a mathematical calculation to offset the images from one another.

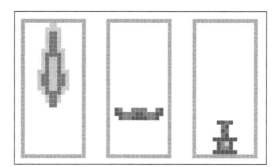

Weapon modules in their respective bounding boxes

Setting the bounding box to an appropriate size will be done in Unity, but we need to make sure that there is adequate room in the sprite sheet to do this. We have been using the metric to indicate that each of our tiles is 32 x 32 pixels. We will want to place our modules within a tile of this size so that each module occupies the same amount of space.

We will be making four modules for each sword component, which means four blades, four hilts, and four handles. This is a total of 12 modules. We can space them out to make four 32 pixel columns by three 32 pixel rows. The exact size of this sprite sheet is 128 pixels (width) by 96 pixels (height). Even though we are using a low-resolution art form, we can still match pixels in this same way for any 2D resolution art modulation.

The sprite sheet, which is provided to you in the accompanying files of `Chapter 6`, uses a blade height of 21 pixels. In each 32 pixel block, you can align the top of the blade with the top of the canvas. Then, you will align the top of the hilt to be just under 22 pixels from the top of a different block.

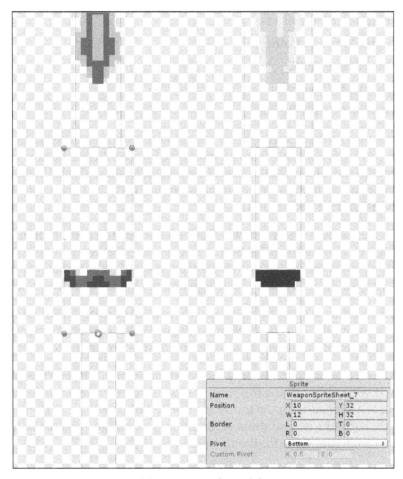

Measurements of a module

Once our sprite sheet is prepared and ready for use, we will import it into our Unity project under the **Sprites** folder, as we did earlier. Here are the steps as a reminder:

1. Inside the Unity Editor, navigate to the **Project** tab.

2. Open the **Sprites** folder, right-click and select **Import New Asset…**.

3. Navigate to your modular weapon sprite sheet; the one provided is named `WeaponSpriteSheet.png`.

We will now have to do some Unity-specific editing. We will be setting the sprite settings to what we were using in the previous chapters. The sprite import settings are as follows:

1. Set **Sprite Mode** to **Multiple**.
2. Set **Pixels Per Unit** to `32`.
3. Set **Filter Mode** to **Point**.
4. Set **Max Size** to **1024**.
5. Set **Format** to **Truecolor**.
6. Click on the **Apply** button.

After you are done with the settings, we are going to slice the sprites so that they will overlap correctly. Each sprite will contain the image of its respective module and some transparent space for the other component to show through. Also, we have to consider an animation to swing the weapon. It will be beneficial to set a common pivot point for each module.

With `WeaponSpriteSheet.png` selected, click on the **Sprite Editor** button in the **Inspector** tab. You can try the **Slice** button in the upper-left corner of the **Sprite Editor** window, but some of these modules are too small for it to easily detect. Either way, you will have to make some adjustments to the bounding box.

You can click and drag a bounding box anywhere in the **Sprite Editor** window. Once a bounding box is made, you can click and drag one of its corners to change its size. You will see the size of the currently selected bounding box in the lower-right corner.

You can make each bounding box only the width of the module, but the height must be 32 pixels. If you start with the top row, you can drag the boxes that are 32 pixels in height and are aligned with the top of the **Sprite Editor** window. Then, you can move on to the second row and draw similar boxes that align with the bottom of the top row. You can do the same for the third row.

We will also set the pivot point to be the same for each module so that it can rotate for our animation at the same point. The pivot point is the center circle of each box and can be dragged and dropped anywhere. We want it at the very bottom of every bounding box.

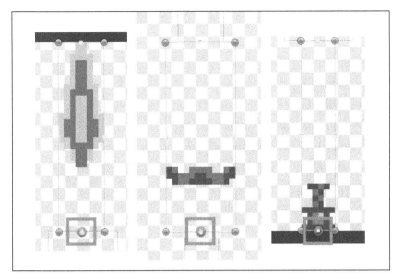

Pivot points for each type of module

When you are done, you can click on **Accept** in the upper-right corner of the Sprite Editor. The WeaponSpriteSheet.png file should now have an arrow on it, showing that you can expand it to see the separated modules. We are now ready to make our Weapon prefab.

# Creating a multiple image prefab

Unity GameObjects can only hold one Sprite Renderer component at a time. This Sprite Renderer can only render one sprite at a time. So, the easiest way to achieve our goal is to make multiple GameObjects, each with their own Sprite Renderer. We can then place all the module GameObjects under a parent GameObject for easy reference.

A more optimal solution would be to have the module sprites redrawn as a single sprite and then passed to a single Sprite Renderer in a single GameObject. GameObjects are rather large structures, and too many of them can impact performance. For now, our solution will work fine, but perhaps, you can return to this issue later and find a way to compress everything into a single GameObject.

We will start making our Weapon prefab with an empty GameObject with the following steps:

1. Create a new empty GameObject.
2. Name the GameObject `Weapon`.
3. Add a tag to the GameObject called `Weapon` as well.
4. Put the **Weapon** object in the **Units** layer.
5. Add a **Box Collider 2D** component.
6. In **Box Collider 2D**, check **Is Trigger**.
7. Create another empty GameObject.
8. Name the new empty GameObject `WeaponComponents1`.
9. Put the **WeaponComponents1** object in the **Units** layer.
10. Add a **Sprite Renderer** component.
11. Put **Sorting Layer** of the **Sprite Renderer** component to the **Units** layer.
12. Drag and drop the **WeaponComponents1** object into the **Weapon** object to make it a child of the **Weapon** object.
13. You can then duplicate the **WeaponComponents1** object twice, and name them `WeaponComponents2` and `WeaponComponents3`.

At this point, we have done all that we can for the creation of the prefab. We need to add some scripts now that will configure the modular weapon behind the scenes, much like we did with the random items in *Chapter 5, Randomized Items*. So, let's take a look at the weapon and weapon component scripts.

# Modular weapon scripts

Our modular weapon script will do the following three main actions:

- The `Weapon` script will create the connection to the player and the weapon
- The player will need to carry and use the weapon
- The script will drive the scripted animation, and it will also drive the random construction of the weapon from the weapon component

We are going to place some hooks in the class definition as empty functions that we will fill in when we have some more information. Let's take a look at the full `Weapon` class script that's shown in *Code Snip 6.1*:

```
1 using UnityEngine;
2 using System.Collections;
3
```

```
4 public class Weapon : MonoBehaviour {
5
6  public bool inPlayerInventory = false;
7
8  private Player player;
9  private WeaponComponents[] weaponsComps;
10 private bool weaponUsed = false;
11
12  public void AcquireWeapon () {}
13
14  void Update () {}
15
16  public void useWeapon () {}
17
18  public void enableSpriteRender (bool isEnabled) {}
19
20  public Sprite getComponentImage (int index) {
21     return null;
22  }
23 }
```

Let's go through and explain what's happening in the Weapon class script:

- Line 6: inPlayerInventory is a Boolean flag to identify whether or not the weapon was picked up by the player.

- Line 8: We want to keep a reference to the player character so that we can provide a reference to its absolute position at all times.

- Line 9: We will have an array of references to the weapon components child.

- Line 10: weaponUsed is another flag that we will use to trigger the swing animation.

- Line 12: This is our first hook. AcquireWeapon will be the function that the Player class calls in order to add a weapon to the inventory. We will need to make the Weapon class a child of the Player class as well.

- Line 14: We are keeping the Update() function because we will be running an animation that's controlled in this script. The animation will have to update frames along with the timing of the game.

- Line 16: useWeapon() will be the function that is called by the player to start the weapon swing animation.

- Line 18: Because the `Weapon` class is a child of the `Player` class and is always in the same location as the `Player` class, we will need a way to make it invisible. `enableSpriteRender (bool isEnabled)` will disable the Sprite Renderers of the weapon components to keep them invisible till they are used.

- Line 20: We want to inform the player about the weapon that they are carrying. Like the glove and boot items, we will add on a screen image of the sword that the player currently has in his or her inventory. `getComponentImage (int index)` will get the image that's to be displayed on the screen.

We will return to the `Weapon` class definition throughout the rest of this chapter as we discover what is required to make our `Weapon` class work. We will follow the `Weapon` class definition with the `WeaponComponents` class definition. We will then be able to fill in some of the blanks from the `Weapon` class definition. After all this, we can finish constructing the **Weapon** prefab. For now, let's take a look at the `WeaponComponents` class in *Code Snip 6.2*:

```
1 using UnityEngine;
2 using System.Collections;
3 using Random = UnityEngine.Random;
4
5 public class WeaponComponents : MonoBehaviour {
6
7   public Sprite[] modules;
8
9   private Weapon parent;
10 private SpriteRenderer spriteRenderer;
11
12  void Start () {
13    parent = GetComponentInParent<Weapon> ();
14    spriteRenderer = GetComponent<SpriteRenderer> ();
15    spriteRenderer.sprite = modules [Random.Range(0,
      modules.Length)];
16  }
17
18  void Update () {
19    transform.eulerAngles = parent.transform.eulerAngles;
20  }
```

```
21
22  public SpriteRenderer getSpriteRenderer () {
23    return spriteRenderer;
24  }
25 }
```

We will be able to choose which modules we want this component to render in the Unity Editor. The array of modules that we give the `WeaponComponent` class will have a single module that's chosen from it to be rendered. Let's take a look at what we have developed in *Code Snip 6.2*:

- `Line 3`: Set `Random` to use the Unity built-in Random library.

- `Line 7`: This array will hold the different modules that make up a weapon.

- `Line 9`: We will need to store a reference to the `parent` object, which is the `Weapon` object. The `Weapon` script will direct our weapon components to turn off and on.

- `Line 10`: We will also need to store a reference to the Sprite Renderer component to turn it off and on.

- `Lines 12-16`: The `Start()` function will be where we set up our parent and Sprite Renderer references. The function will then randomly select the module from the array of modules to render.

- `Lines 18-20`: We will use the `Update()` function to continuously poll the `parent` weapon object for it's angle. We want all of the weapon components to match the angle of the `parent` weapon object and, in turn, the player character. The plan is to turn the weapon as the player character turns.

- `Lines 22-24`: We want to pass a reference to the component's Sprite Renderer. This way, we can manipulate when the Sprite Renderer is enabled or disabled in the `Weapon` class.

Now that we have the `WeaponComponent` class written, we can finish building our Weapon prefab. Return to the Unity Editor, and select the **Weapon** GameObject in the `Hierarchy` panel. Add the `Weapon.cs` script.

Next, select each weapon component GameObject that is a child of the **Weapon** GameObject. Add the `WeaponComponents.cs` script. Then, for **WeaponComponents1**, select the **Modules** array and set the size to 4. Add the corresponding blade module sprites. Do the same for the other weapon components.

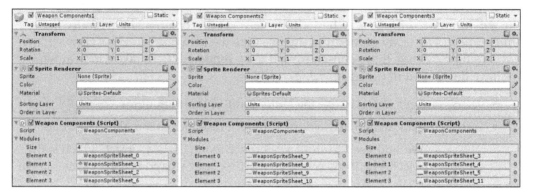

Weapon Component's settings

You can now drag and drop the whole **Weapon** prefab into the **Prefabs** folder, and delete the **Weapon** object from the **Hierarchy** panel. You'll see that the **Weapon** prefab can be expanded. If you expand it, you'll see the child prefabs that are the weapon components. You can edit the individual components here:

The expanded Weapon prefab

# Adding a spawn point

Now that we have our Weapon prefab put together, we are going to need a way to get it to the player. We've already answered this problem, with the chest, in the previous chapter. We will just reuse the Chest object to also spawn weapons as well.

Open the Chest.cs script that's to be edited. We will want to add a variable to store a reference to our generated weapon. Add the `public Weapon weapon;` variable right under our `randomItem` variable. Then, we need to make some adjustments to our Open() function, which can be seen in *Code Snip 6.3*:

```
1 public void Open () {
2   spriteRenderer.sprite = openSprite;
3
4   GameObject toInstantiate;
5
6   if (Random.Range (0, 2) == 1) {
7     randomItem.RandomItemInit ();
8     toInstantiate = randomItem.gameObject;
9   } else {
10     toInstantiate = weapon.gameObject;
11   }
12   GameObject instance = Instantiate (toInstantiate, new Vector3
      (transform.position.x, transform.position.y, 0f),
      Quaternion.identity) as GameObject;
13   instance.transform.SetParent (transform.parent);
14   gameObject.layer = 10;
15   spriteRenderer.sortingLayerName = "Items";
16 }
```

This will be a pretty simple update. We just need to add the condition that weapons can spawn as well. Let's take a look at how this can be done:

- Lines 6-11: We add the new random conditional here. Right now, items and weapons have a 50/50 chance that either will spawn, but you can experiment with this value as you see fit.

- Lines 12-15: We pushed the actual instantiation call to the bottom of the function so that we could either instantiate an item or weapon, but we don't really need to explicitly know which is which.

Returning to the Unity Editor, go to the **Chest** prefab, and in the **Chest Script** component, assign the **Weapon** prefab to the **Weapon** field. Now you can play the game and check that the chest spawns a randomized modular weapon. By interacting with some chests, you should eventually find a sword. You won't be able to pick the weapon up like you did with items, but this completes the first step.

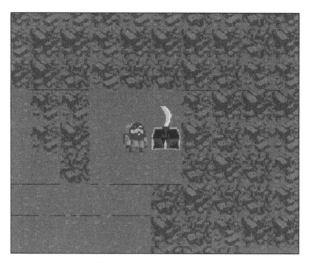

Chest spawning a weapon

# Adding a weapon pick up

Now, we can move on to adding the logic that will run the player pickup of the weapon object. This will be very similar to the other player pickups except that the weapon will need a few special considerations. For one, the weapon will need to be in the same screen location as the player at all times so that it can animate appropriately.

Let's begin by opening up the Player.cs script where the current player pickup logic exists. We are going to add a few new variables that will hold references to our weapon and some of the images that we will use to make the display icon. As stated earlier, we will create a display icon on the screen that will show the weapon that the player has in their inventory. Add the following lines to the beginning of the Player class definition:

```
1 private Weapon weapon;
2 public Image weaponComp1, weaponComp2, weaponComp3;
```

We will then edit the OnTriggerEnter2D function. We need to add a condition that will allow us to handle against colliding with a weapon object. The updated function can be seen in *Code Snip 6.5*:

```
 1 private void OnTriggerEnter2D (Collider2D other) {
 2  if (other.tag == "Exit") {
 3    dungeonTransition = true;
 4    Invoke ("GoDungeonPortal", 0.5f);
 5    Destroy (other.gameObject);
 6  } else if (other.tag == "Food" || other.tag == "Soda") {
 7    UpdateHealth(other);
 8    Destroy (other.gameObject);
 9  } else if (other.tag == "Item") {
10    UpdateInventory(other);
11    Destroy (other.gameObject);
12  } else if (other.tag == "Weapon") {
13    if (weapon) {
14      Destroy(transform.GetChild(0).gameObject);
15    }
16    other.enabled = false;
17    other.transform.parent = transform;
18    weapon = other.GetComponent<Weapon>();
19    weapon.AcquireWeapon();
20    weapon.inPlayerInventory = true;
21    weapon.enableSpriteRender(false);
22    wallDamage = attackMod + 3;
23    weaponComp1.sprite = weapon.getComponentImage(0);
24    weaponComp2.sprite = weapon.getComponentImage(1);
25    weaponComp3.sprite = weapon.getComponentImage(2);
26
27  }
28 }
```

We aren't adding the weapon object to our inventory map so that we can manipulate it more easily. We can simply change the colors of an existing object, like we did with the items of the previous chapter. Instead, we need to keep track of whether we have a weapon or not before we add another to our player. Let's take a look at what we have developed in *Code Snip 6.5*:

- Line 12: This line starts the conditional statement that checks whether we have collided with a weapon.

- Lines 13-15: We need to check whether we already have a weapon and destroy it if we do. The weapon will get added to the player as a child. The new weapon only overwrites the weapon reference, not the entire GameObject. If we don't remove it, we will end up adding a bunch of objects to the scene that are not used and will potentially slow our game.

- Line 16: We want to disable BoxCollider2D of the spawned weapon so that we don't trigger it again. Remember that the weapon will share the same coordinates as the player.

- Line 17: Here, we make the player the parent of the weapon that we just collided with.

- Line 18: We need to store a reference to the Weapon script.

- Lines 19-21: We will also call all of the functions that initialize the weapon as part of the player inventory. The AcquireWeapon and enableSpriteRender functions haven't been implemented yet, but we will be getting to them shortly.

- Line 22: Adding in attackMod that's brought in by items, we finally get to update the damage done by the player.

- Lines 23-25: Lastly, we are going to update the Image variables so that we can use them for the display icon.

Before we leave the Player class, we should also update the UpdateInventory function. Add the following conditional statement at the end of the function definition:

```
1 if (weapon)
2    wallDamage = attackMod + 3;
```

This additional code will make it so the damage done by the player is recalculated to reflect the newly acquired items and/or weapon.

We can return to the Unity Editor now and check that things are working as we expect them to. Play the game and find a sword spawned from a chest. We couldn't interact with the weapon before, but now we can. Unfortunately, the weapon never hides from view and the display icon is a blank white.

The weapon is unhidden and follows the player, while there is a blank image to the right

We will have to head back to our `Weapon` class definition and start filling out the hook functions that we created. The first of these will be the `AcquireWeapon` function, which is used to initialize the connection between the `Player`, `Weapon`, and `WeaponComponents` classes. We can see the function implementation in *Code Snip 6.6*:

```
1 public void AquireWeapon () {
2    player = GetComponentInParent<Player> ();
3    weaponsComps = GetComponentsInChildren<WeaponComponents> ();
4 }
```

`Line 2` grabs a reference to the `Player` script that the `Weapon` class is attached to. `Line 3` grabs an array of the `WeaponComponents` scripts that are attached to the `Weapon` class. And now the three classes can communicate with each other.

Next is the `enableSpriteRender` function. This function will enable or disable the Sprite Renderers of the `WeaponComponents` class. We can see the function implementation in *Code Snip 6.7*:

```
1 public void enableSpriteRender (bool isEnabled) {
2    foreach (WeaponComponents comp in weaponsComps) {
3       comp.getSpriteRenderer ().enabled = isEnabled;
4    }
5 }
```

We pass a `bool` argument that will represent whether we want to enable or disable the Sprite Renderer. `isEnabled` should be `true` to enable the Sprite Renderer and `false` otherwise. The function uses a loop to call the `getSpriteRenderer` function from each weapon component and sets the returned Sprite Renderer to the value of `isEnabled`.

Lastly, we will use the `getComponentImage` function to return a reference to the weapon component's module sprite. This sprite will then be used by the `Player` class to construct the display icon that will tell us which weapon we are using. The function just needs the `return null;` line to be replaced with the following:

```
return weaponsComps[index].getSpriteRenderer().sprite;
```

With this piece of code, you can save your changes and head back to the Unity Editor. We have completed the spawn and pick up phase of the weapon implementation. You can test it by finding a sword in a chest and walking over it. The sword should disappear from the chest and reappear in the lower-right corner of the screen as part of the UI:

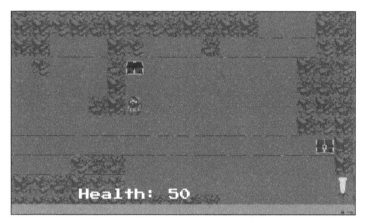

The sword is hidden and the icon to the right appears

After you've checked to see that the weapon pick up is successful, you can find a wall to hit. The wall will sustain more damage and be destroyed quicker, but it is only implied that the sword is causing this effect. It would be more immersive if we could see the sword swing as the player character swipes at the wall.

# Adding scripted weapon animation

The art we imported for our weapon modules is static, which means that we didn't add in any supplemental art to create animations. If we had added in these animations, our art assets would have increased dramatically, and we are trying to avoid this. So, instead, we are going to do what we have been doing and rely on programming.

We want the randomly constructed weapon to animate a swing when the player attacks. So, we are going to program the animation in such a way that it is the same for all the Weapons. This process is very much based on experimentation to get the right look and feel. One solution can be seen in *Code Snip 6.8*. The code is in the Weapon class definition as the Update function definition:

```
1 void Update () {
2   if (inPlayerInventory) {
3     transform.position = player.transform.position;
```

```
4      if (weaponUsed == true) {
5         float degreeY = 0, degreeZ = -90f, degreeZMax = 275f;
6         Vector3 returnVecter = Vector3.zero;
7
8         transform.rotation = Quaternion.Slerp
          (transform.rotation, Quaternion.Euler (0, degreeY,
          degreeZ), Time.deltaTime * 20f);
9         if (transform.eulerAngles.z <= degreeZMax) {
10          transform.eulerAngles = returnVecter;
11          weaponUsed = false;
12          enableSpriteRender (false);
13        }
14      }
15   }
16 }
```

The weapon is initially in an upright state. So, the basics of the animation include making the weapon appear and swing downward from its pivot point. This is the reason we took time to adjust the pivot point of each sprite in the first place. Let's take a look at the scripted animation in *Code Snip 6.8*:

- Line 2: In order for the animation cycle to begin, the player must first have a weapon in his or her inventory. The Player class will directly change the inPlayerInventory variable.

- Line 3: We ensure the weapon shared the same coordinates as the player.

- Line 4: Only when the weaponUsed flag is set, we run the animation cycle. The useWeapon function will be called by the Player class who will set this flag.

- Lines 5-6: These are the various rotation values that need to take place. These values can be adjusted for different arc animations.

- Line 8: This is the actual animation. We use a Slerp function to rotate the sword that originates from the Player class. **Slerp** stands for **spherical linear interpolation**, which is built into Unity.

- Lines 9-13: We only want the sword to swing to a certain angle and then disappear again. Here, we check whether it has exceeded this angle and then, if so, we reset the angle of the weapon.

 For more information on **Slerp (Spherical Linear Interpolation)** in Unity3D, refer to http://docs.unity3d.com/ ScriptReference/Quaternion.Slerp.html.

The animation is fairly simple, but most of the angles were acquired via experimenting and seeing what looked good. Animation usually involves some experimentation with what looks correct to the eye, regardless of your medium. You should play with the values and see what kind of animations you can make as well.

We aren't done with the animation implementation quite yet though. We need a way to drive the animation. The useWeapon function needs its definition filled so that the player can call the weapon animation. The useWeapon function only needs the following two lines:

```
1 enableSpriteRender(true);
2 weaponUsed = true;
```

Now, we need to jump over to the Player class to write in where and when the weapon animation is called. Luckily, this is a very small change as well. In the Player class's OnCantMove function, we will add the following two lines at the end of the function definition:

```
1 if (weapon) {
2   weapon.useWeapon ();
3 }
```

This conditional statement checks whether there is a weapon in the player's inventory and if there is, then the Player class will call the animation. Note that the OnCantMove function is called when there is something obstructing the player's path. Therefore, the weapon animation will only be called when an object is obstructing the player's path, such as a wall or an enemy.

Go back to the Unity Editor to try out the newly implemented weapon animation. You'll need to go find a sword, exit the dungeon, and then attack a wall tile. If you attack a wall that is to the right of the player, you'll see the animation as if the player swings the sword at and through the wall.

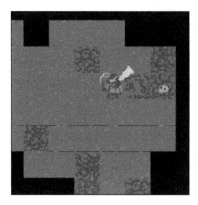

Weapon animation

If you attack a wall that is to the left of the player, the player still swings to the right. In addition to this, the player is permanently facing toward the right. This just doesn't look right and pulls the player out of the immersion, as follows:

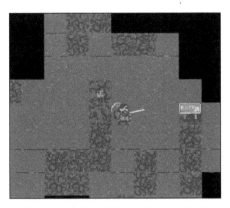

The player faces to the right and the sword swings to the right as well, while the wall on the left is damaged

# Adding character facing directions

The last task we have is to add a functionality that will allow the player to change the direction he or she faces. Then, we can add some functionality that will allow the sword to swing in the same direction that the player is facing. To achieve this, we will have to start in the MovingObject class.

The AttempMove function is where the direction of the player is managed. This is where we can poll what direction the player is moving in, and change the sprite direction accordingly. *Code snip 6.9* shows the update that should be added to the top of the AttemptMove function definition:

```
1 protected virtual bool AttemptMove <T> (int xDir, int yDir)
2   where T : Component
3 {
4   if (xDir == 1) {
5     transform.eulerAngles = Vector3.zero;
6   } else if (xDir == -1) {
7     transform.eulerAngles = new Vector3(0,180,0);
8   }
...
```

The AttemptMove function was initially written with the integers representing the direction that the player is moving in. If xDir is 1, then the player moves to the right of the screen, and if xDir is -1, the player moves to the left. This is reminiscent of a coordinate plane.

So, in `lines 4-8`, we write a conditional statement that states when the player is headed to the right, we set the transform rotation to `0`. If the player is headed to the left, then we rotate the player sprite 180 degrees on the *y* axis. This will flip the sprite so that it faces the left of the screen. When the player is headed to the right, it will flip back to the origin. The following screenshot shows our player character, who at first, only faced right and now faces left:

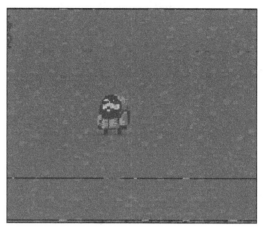

The player can now face left

You can head back to the Unity Editor and check this work correctly. But if you obtain a weapon and try to use it while facing left, it will still swing to the right. So, we need to do a little more work to correct the swing of the weapon.

First, we need to add some functionality to the `Weapon` class. In the `Update` function where the animation takes place, we will need to add a condition in which the weapon can swing to the left. *Code snip 6.10* shows the necessary changes that need to be made to the `Weapon` class's `Update` function:

```
1 void Update () {
2   if (inPlayerInventory) {
3     transform.position = player.transform.position;
4     if (weaponUsed == true) {
5       float degreeY = 0, degreeZ = -90f, degreeZMax = 275f;
6       Vector3 returnVecter = Vector3.zero;
7       if (Player.isFacingRight) {
8         degreeY = 0;
9         returnVecter = Vector3.zero;
```

```
10          } else if (!Player.isFacingRight) {
11            degreeY = 180;
12            returnVecter = new Vector3(0,180,0);
13          }
14          transform.rotation = Quaternion.Slerp
            (transform.rotation, Quaternion.Euler (0, degreeY,
            degreeZ), Time.deltaTime * 20f);
15          if (transform.eulerAngles.z <= degreeZMax) {
16            transform.eulerAngles = returnVecter;
17            weaponUsed = false;
18            enableSpriteRender (false);
19          }
20        }
21    }
22  }
```

Lines 7-14 are the new additions. We add a conditional statement that checks whether the player is facing to the right or not. We use a `bool` variable that doesn't exist yet, but we will add this to the `Player` class definition shortly. The conditional statement changes the rotation of the *y* axis via `degreeY`, which will make the weapon face toward the right or left, like the player does. Then, it sets the value that will return the weapon to it's upright starting position relative to the direction that it faces.

Once this is complete, we can move on to the `Player` class definition and make some final changes there. At the top of the `Player` class definition, add the `public static bool isFacingRight;` line. This variable is the one we refer to in the Weapon class to determine the direction that the player faces.

Next, we need to actually set the value for the `isFacingRight` variable. This will take place in the `Player` class override of the `AttemptMove` function. At the top of the function definition, add this conditional statement:

```
1 if (xDir == 1 && !isFacingRight) {
2   isFacingRight = true;
3 } else if (xDir == -1 && isFacingRight) {
4   isFacingRight = false;
5 }
```

Save your changes and head back to the Unity Editor. You can test the newly completed weapon system. Your character now turns to the left and right as well and swings his or her weapon in the correct direction. You can see this best if you find and use the asymmetrical curved sword.

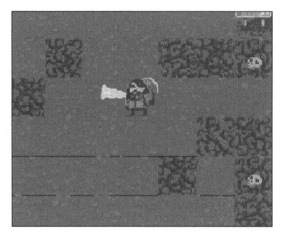

The player can swing the sword toward the left

The sword now swings to the left and right, but what about upward and downward? Our character can attack in four directions and we have only handled two of them. This is a good exercise for you to tackle on your own. Try adding a sword animation that arcs the sword above the player's head and below his or her feet.

# Summary

This completes the implementation of modular weapons. Remember that for our weapon prefab, all you need to do is add another set of three modules (blade, hilt, and handle) to drastically increase the number of combinations that the Weapon prefab can take. We did more than just create a useless modular weapon, though; we actually implemented its full functionality. This gave us some insight on a few different development techniques, such as scripted animation.

In this chapter, you learned about what a modular weapon is and the concept of breaking a structure down to small reusable parts. You learned that a few additional modules can create exponentially more combinations. We also developed one technique in procedurally generating and combining sprites to make a whole GameObject. Lastly, you developed a system to animate the weapon action via a script alone.

There are some optimizations that can be made with this system that I will leave up to you. Remember, every GameObject we add to the screen will slow down the entire game and is very hard to enable on mobile platforms. I recommend that you look into how you might combine modules into one sprite, and then add a single GameObject instead of four per weapon.

Next, we are going to put those weapons and items to use as we introduce enemies with adaptive difficulty. We can procedurally change and adapt our AI and enemy strength to the player as they get stronger in the game.

# 7
# Adaptive Difficulty

In *Chapter 2*, *Roguelike Games*, we imported an Enemy prefab and an Enemy script but we haven't used either of them yet. So far, our character has been wandering around an empty world collecting food and items. But that is all about to change because in this chapter, we are going to add brain hungry zombies that scale in difficulty and test the player's strength.

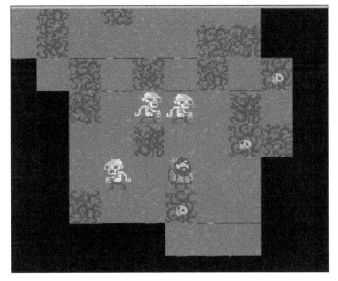

Player among enemies!

Adaptive difficulty can be solely a PCG solution or it can, in part, rely on an **artificial intelligence (AI)** solution. Our main goal with PCG is to expand the playtime and game content. Normally, when we think of PCG, we think of content such as art assets being programmatically created or new game objects being added to the game at runtime. We can also think of PCG as a means to expand the game's complexity internally as well.

We will be adding enemies to both the world board and Dungeon Board. At first, the enemies won't be very dangerous as they are slow and not good at navigating obstacles. However, as the player gains weapons and items and becomes more dangerous, the enemies will get smarter, faster, and more numerous.

In this chapter, you will be learning how to use the idea of PCG to change the gameplay and make it more challenging. You will develop some simple AI and path-finding routines. Then, lastly, you will adjust the AI during gameplay to keep the player challenged. We will cover the following topics:

- Adding enemies to the world board
- Adding enemies to the Dungeon Board
- Fighting the enemy
- Adaptive difficulty

So, we will be generating enemies for the player to battle against, but we will also be generating the enemy's behavior. The goal is to increase the challenge the player faces as the player gets stronger. Making the enemies stronger as well does really change how the game is played, but making the enemies smarter will shift game play and challenge the player mentally, which should make for a more entertaining game.

The distinction between AI and PCG is, PCG is used to manipulate or generate content and AI is a programmed behavior set. We then use PCG to manipulate the AI as if it were content. In the example later in the chapter, you will see that we add new AI behaviors as our player progresses.

# Setting up sprites

We will now add enemy scripts and set up sprites.

First on our agenda is setting up the Enemy prefab and script. Let's take a look at the Enemy prefab. The prefab was imported with all of the starting materials in `Chapter 2`. Just in case you need an extra copy of the Enemy prefab though, there will be an import file in the accompanying `Chapter 7` files.

The Enemy prefab looks a lot like the Player prefab. Both the `Enemy` and `Player` classes inherit from the `Moving Object` class. This means the enemy movement and animations are going to be processed in a similar way to the `Player` class. This generally means the prefab structure will have to be similar.

Enemy Sprite

Requirements for our Enemy prefab include:

- A Sprite Renderer
- An Animator
- A Box Collider 2D
- A Rigid Body 2D
- The Enemy Script

Also, be sure that these options are selected in your Enemy prefab:

- Set the tag to **Enemy**
- Set the layer to **BlockingLayer**
- In the **Sprite Renderer** component, set the **Sorting Layer** field to **Units**
- In the **Animator** component, set the **Controller** field to use the **Enemy Animator Controller**

That's it for the Enemy prefab. All the magic is going to happen in the Enemy script. Go ahead and open the Enemy script for editing. You will see the following lines:

```
1 using UnityEngine;
2 using System.Collections;
3
4 public class Enemy : MovingObject
5 {
6   protected override bool AttemptMove <T> (int xDir, int yDir)
7   {
8     return true;
9   }
10
11  protected override void OnCantMove <T> (T component)
12  {
13  }
14 }
```

The `Enemy` script is currently a placeholder. The movement cycle in the game is turn based. The player needs to play a turn by moving and only then is it the enemy's turn, and back to the player in a cycle. We added the `enemy` class at the beginning of our *Roguelike* game so that this turn-based system would be functional from the get go, hence the `Enemy` class placeholder. So, now, all we have to do is add the enemy functionality to the placeholder and the turn-based movement system will work as is.

We can now go ahead and add the enemy base functionality. *Code Snip 7-1* shows what we need to add to get started with enemies in our game. The code snippet includes the movement functionality and what the enemy does when it is blocked from moving. This will be similar to the player's movement. Following the code snippet, we will take a look at the details of the code:

```
1 using UnityEngine;
2 using System.Collections;
3
4 public class Enemy : MovingObject {
5
6    public int playerDamage;
7
8    private Animator animator;
9    private Transform target;
10   private bool skipMove;
11
12   protected override void Start () {
13     GameManager.instance.AddEnemyToList (this);
14
15     animator = GetComponent<Animator> ();
16
17     target = GameObject.FindGameObjectWithTag
          ("Player").transform;
18
19     base.Start ();
20   }
21
22   protected override void AttemptMove <T> (int xDir, int yDir) {
23     if(skipMove) {
24       skipMove = false;
25       return;
26     }
27
28     base.AttemptMove <T> (xDir, yDir);
29
30     skipMove = true;
```

```
31   }
32
33   public void MoveEnemy () {
34      int xDir = 0;
35      int yDir = 0;
36
37      if(Mathf.Abs (target.position.x - transform.position.x) <
         float.Epsilon)
38         yDir = target.position.y > transform.position.y ? 1 : -1;
39      else
40         xDir = target.position.x > transform.position.x ? 1 : -1;
41
42      AttemptMove <Player> (xDir, yDir);
43   }
44
45   protected override void OnCantMove <T> (T component) {
46      Player hitPlayer = component as Player;
47
48      hitPlayer.LoseHealth (playerDamage);
49
50      animator.SetTrigger ("enemyAttack");
51   }
52 }
```

The enemy will try to move towards the player and when the player is adjacent to the enemy the enemy will attack the player. The enemy movement AI is handled in the new MoveEnemy function. We will see how the enemy moves on its own as we go over the code in *Code Snip 7.1*:

- Lines 1-2: The Enemy class only requires UnityEngine and System. Collections.

- Line 4: Be sure to inherit from the MovingObject class.

- Lines 8-10: The starting variable we need to get this class working is an Animator to control the animations, a Transform called target to be the player, and a bool called skipMove to slow the enemy down.

- Line 12: We will add a Start function to initialize everything.

- Line 13: We need to add the enemies to a list so we can keep track of them because there will likely be more than one on screen. The AddEnemyToList function has been in the GameManager class since *Chapter 2, Roguelike Games* but we haven't used it until now. The GameManager class will be in charge of the enemies and run their movement.

- **Line 17**: Here, we set the target to the player. We want the enemies to know the position of the player at all times so that the enemies can chase the player.

- **Lines 22-31**: We are going to expand the `AttemptMove` function and make it so that the enemies aren't as fast as the player to start with. First, we check to see whether the `skipMove` variable is set to `true`, and if it is, we set it back to `false` and exit the function, effectively ending the enemies' turn without movement. If `skipMove` is `false`, then we call the base class `AttemptMove` function.

- **Lines 33-43**: This is a new function that the `GameManager` class will call when it is time to move the enemies. This function contains the AI logic of the `Enemy` class.

- **Lines 34-35**: The goal of the function is to record the direction of the player into $xDir$ and $yDir$. We can only move one space at a time, though, so either $xDir$ or $yDir$ will get the 1/-1 value.

- **Lines 37-40**: The AI is basic. We want the enemy to move in the $x$ direction towards the player. If the player and enemy are on the same $x$ coordinate, then we want the enemy to move toward the enemy in the $y$ direction. We do not take into account that the enemy can easily get stuck on a wall and get blocked from reaching the player. In fact, this is a desired effect as we want the player to be able to escape the enemy at the beginning when the player does very little damage.

- **Line 42**: Once the enemy has a direction, it will call its `AttemptMove` function.

- **Lines 45-51**: Last is our `OnCantMove` function. Our component is going to be the player and if we hit him, then we will call the `Player.LoseHealth` function to reflect the damage. We will also call an enemy attack animation.

Our enemy base functionality is all set up. Of course, that isn't enough. The `Enemy` class won't just move on its own, it needs some other structure to guide it. This structure would be the `GameManager` class. We should also be thinking about what will happen to the enemy once they are on the world board.

It is impossible for our player to walk on the black space surrounding our floor tiles because every step of the player generates new floor tiles. The same isn't true for enemies though. They will be able to walk anywhere unless we write the conditions to constrain them to the board. We will need to keep this under consideration as we spawn enemies on the world board.

Enemy walking on black space

# Adding enemies to the world board

As usual, we will need to generate the enemies at random to keep the player on their toes. We then need to address the issue of enemies being able to move through black space. We will also have to handle the event that an enemy moves off screen.

Let's start by adding the enemies to the world board. Open up the BoardManager. cs script for editing. You can start by adding the line public GameObject enemy; under all the other public variables. This will be our Enemy prefab reference. Then, take a look at *Code Snip 7.2* for the rest of the update:

```
1 private void addTiles(Vector2 tileToAdd) {
2   if (!gridPositions.ContainsKey (tileToAdd)) {
3     gridPositions.Add (tileToAdd, tileToAdd);
4     GameObject toInstantiate = floorTiles [Random.Range (0,
      floorTiles.Length)];
5     GameObject instance = Instantiate (toInstantiate, new Vector3
      (tileToAdd.x, tileToAdd.y, 0f), Quaternion.identity) as
      GameObject;
6     instance.transform.SetParent (boardHolder);
7
8     if (Random.Range (0, 3) == 1) {
9       toInstantiate = wallTiles[Random.Range
        (0,wallTiles.Length)];
10      instance = Instantiate (toInstantiate, new Vector3
        (tileToAdd.x, tileToAdd.y, 0f), Quaternion.identity) as
        GameObject;
```

```
11       instance.transform.SetParent (boardHolder);
12     } else if (Random.Range (0, 50) == 1) {
13       toInstantiate = exit;
14       instance = Instantiate (toInstantiate, new Vector3
         (tileToAdd.x, tileToAdd.y, 0f), Quaternion.identity) as
         GameObject;
15       instance.transform.SetParent (boardHolder);
16     }
17     else if (Random.Range (0, 20) == 1) {
18       toInstantiate = enemy;
19       instance = Instantiate (toInstantiate, new Vector3
         (tileToAdd.x, tileToAdd.y, 0f), Quaternion.identity) as
         GameObject;
20       instance.transform.SetParent (boardHolder);
21     }
22   }
23 }
```

*Code Snip 7.2* shows the full `addTiles` function from the `BoardManager` class with the addition of spawning enemies. `Lines 17-21` show the additional check needed to randomly generate an enemy. So the player will walk and discover new areas of the world board, but just as random wall tiles appear, so too will enemies now.

We still need to handle when and where enemies can move. The simplest and probably the easiest solution to enemies moving over black space is to destroy them if they move into that area. We can piggyback on that idea and also destroy enemies if they move outside of the camera view. This way enemies that are not rendered will not have a turn to move and slow down the overall game.

To implement this functionality open up the `GameManager.cs` script for editing. We will be adding several small functions and updating others. Take a look at *Code Snip 7.3* for the updates:

```
1 public void AddEnemyToList (Enemy script) {
2   enemies.Add (script);
3 }
4
5 public void RemoveEnemyFromList (Enemy script) {
6   enemies.Remove (script);
7 }
8
9 public bool checkValidTile (Vector2 pos) {
10  if (gridPositions.ContainsKey (pos)) {
11    return true;
12  }
```

```
13  return false;
14 }
15
16 IEnumerator MoveEnemies() {
17    enemiesMoving = true;
18
19    yield return new WaitForSeconds(turnDelay);
20
21    if (enemies.Count == 0)  {
22      yield return new WaitForSeconds(turnDelay);
23    }
24
25    List<Enemy> enemiesToDestroy = new List<Enemy>();
26    for (int i = 0; i < enemies.Count; i++) {
27      if ((!enemies[i].getSpriteRenderer().isVisible) ||
         (!boardScript.checkValidTile
         (enemies[i].transform.position))) {
28        enemiesToDestroy.Add(enemies[i]);
29        continue;
30      }
31
32      enemies[i].MoveEnemy ();
33
34      yield return new WaitForSeconds(enemies[i].moveTime);
35    }
36    playersTurn = true;
37    enemiesMoving = false;
38
39    for (int i = 0; i < enemiesToDestroy.Count; i++) {
40      enemies.Remove(enemiesToDestroy[i]);
41      Destroy(enemiesToDestroy[i].gameObject);
42    }
43    enemiesToDestroy.Clear ();
44 }
```

The enemies list will be coming into play now. We add enemies to this list as they are generated, and then, on every move cycle, the GameManager class will loop through the list and move each enemy. Let's take a look at how this is done in the code:

- Lines 1-3: First, we need to define an AddEnemyToList function. This will be called by the Enemy class when an enemy is spawned.

- Lines 5-7: Next, we need to define a RemoveEnemyFromList function. We will call this whenever an enemy is destroyed by the player defeating it.

- Line 9-14: The newly added checkValidTile function will take the position of an enemy and check to see whether that position is in the dictionary of visible floor tiles.

- Lines 16-43: Here, we have our definition for the MoveEnemies function. This function is a coroutine and is therefore declared to have the IEnumerator return type.

- Line 17: We want to prevent the player from moving while the enemies are moving, so we set the flag enemiesMoving. We will deactivate said flag after all the enemies are done with their movement.

- Line 18: We'll wait one increment of turnDelay with yield return regardless of how many enemies need to move.

- Lines 21-23: Next, we will run a check to make sure we have enemies in our list to move. If not, then we make the player wait one more increment of turnDelay. This second turn delay is to make the player wait the amount of time it would take a single onscreen enemy to move. If you add it up, the minimum move time is 0.2 seconds, which is just an arbitrary value that looks and feels adequate during game play.

- Line 25: enemiesToDestroy will be a secondary list that will track the enemies that we need to remove from the game after their move is completed. Directly removing enemies from the enemies list while in a loop might result in our loop trying to access items that are no longer there. So instead, we will use a separate list to help us keep track of our destroyed enemies.

- Lines 26-35: The for loop will cycle through all our onscreen enemies and begin by checking whether they are visible to the camera and that they are standing on a valid tile. If either of those are false, then that enemy is placed in the enemiesToDestroy list and the loop starts with the next iteration. Otherwise, the enemy moves a single space and waits for the normal turn delay.

- Lines 36-37: After the enemy movement is complete, we reset the playerTurn and enemiesMoving flags so the player has control again.

- Lines 39-43: Lastly, we loop through the enemiesToDestroy list and remove enemies from the enemies list. We also destroy those GameObjects. Then, we clear the enemiesToDestroy list just to make sure it takes up no more memory.

And that should do it for our enemy and world board spawning implementation. We can give this a test simply by playing the game. Enemies should randomly spawn in new revealed areas and attempt to move towards the player. They should also permanently vanish if they move completely off screen or into the black outer area.

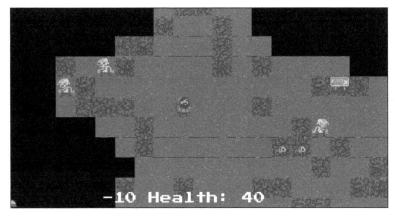

Enemies on world board

Still, no place is safe for the player. We want to also spawn enemies on the Dungeon Board that we generated in *Chapter 4*, *Generating Random Dungeons*. This will pose a different challenge as the dungeon is a fixed, enclosed area. There will be no black space accessible to the enemies and it wouldn't make as much sense to delete them when they move off screen.

# Adding enemies to the Dungeon Board

There are a few things to consider when switching to the Dungeon Board and spawning new enemies. First, we need to determine what will happen when the enemies are off screen. On the world board, we simply destroyed the enemies. We can justify this action because new enemies will be generated as the player discovers new tiles on the world board. However, the player doesn't generate new tiles with movement in the dungeon.

For simplicity, we'll want to generate the dungeon enemies at the same time we generate the dungeon. This means that most enemies generated in a dungeon are generated off screen. If we kept the same offscreen check we had for the world board, we would end up generating enemies and then destroying most of them before the player had a turn to move. Instead, we'll just disable the movement of offscreen enemies while in the dungeon.

We will also have to figure out what to do with the enemies left on the world board when we enter the dungeon and vice versa. In order to keep the number of enemies that we track to a minimum, it might be in our best interest to destroy enemies left on the world board as we enter a dungeon. And since we cannot re-enter a dungeon once we exit, it makes sense that we destroy all the enemies left in a dungeon as we return to the world board.

So, now that we have a plan, let's implement the functionality that will spawn enemies in our dungeons. We can begin with the DungeonManager class so open the DungeonManager.cs file for editing. *Code-Snip 7.4* shows the changes needed for this feature:

```
1 public enum TileType {
2   essential, random, empty, chest, enemy
3 }
4
5 private void BuildRandomPath () {
...

6          if (!gridPositions.ContainsKey(newRPathPos)) {
7            if (Random.Range (0, 20) == 1) {
8              gridPositions.Add (newRPathPos, TileType.enemy);
9            } else {
10             gridPositions.Add (newRPathPos, TileType.empty);
11           }
12
13           PathTile newRPath = new PathTile (TileType.random,
              newRPathPos, minBound, maxBound, gridPositions);
14           pathQueue.Add (newRPath);
15         }
16       }
17     }
18   });
19 }
```

In *Code Snip 7.4*, we first add the enumeration enemy to TileType. We use this enumeration to discern information about the format of our generated dungeon. Then, we make a small change to the BuildRandomPath function. Take note that the full BuildRandomPath function is not present in *Code Snip 7.4*:

- Lines 7-10: We add another condition that gives us the chance to place a tile marked as TileType enemy. The BoardManager class will see this tile and place an enemy on it.

That's all for the `DungeonManager` class. We added a new `TileType` though, and those are also used by the `BoardManager` class to place tile on the boards. So let's open the `BoardManager.cs` script for editing. *Code Snip 7.5* shows the change needed to handle the enemy `TileType` enum:

```
1  public void SetDungeonBoard (Dictionary<Vector2,TileType>
   dungeonTiles, int bound, Vector2 endPos) {
2    boardHolder.gameObject.SetActive (false);
3    dungeonBoardHolder = new GameObject ("Dungeon").transform;
4    GameObject toInstantiate, instance;
5
6    foreach(KeyValuePair<Vector2,TileType> tile in dungeonTiles) {
7      toInstantiate = floorTiles [Random.Range (0,
       floorTiles.Length)];
8      instance = Instantiate (toInstantiate, new Vector3
       (tile.Key.x, tile.Key.y, 0f), Quaternion.identity) as
       GameObject;
9      instance.transform.SetParent (dungeonBoardHolder);
10
11     if (tile.Value == TileType.chest) {
12       toInstantiate = chestTile;
13       instance = Instantiate (toInstantiate, new Vector3
         (tile.Key.x, tile.Key.y, 0f), Quaternion.identity) as
         GameObject;
14       instance.transform.SetParent (dungeonBoardHolder);
15     }
16     else if (tile.Value == TileType.enemy) {
17       toInstantiate = enemy;
18       instance = Instantiate (toInstantiate, new Vector3
         (tile.Key.x, tile.Key.y, 0f), Quaternion.identity) as
         GameObject;
19       instance.transform.SetParent (dungeonBoardHolder);
20     }
21   }
   ...
```

The only change we need to make will take place in the `SetDungeonBoard` function. Note that *Code Snip 7.5* does not show the whole function. On `lines 16-20`, we will need to check whether the tile has spawned an enemy and if so, we place that enemy on the board.

Lastly, we need to run everything in the `GameManager` class. We will be handling where the enemies are spawned and when they are cleaned up here. Go ahead and open the `GameManager.cs` script for editing. *Code Snip 7.6* shows the changes we will be making:

```
1 private bool playerInDungeon;
2
3 void InitGame() {
4   enemies.Clear();
5   boardScript.BoardSetup();
6   playerInDungeon = false;
7 }
8
9 IEnumerator MoveEnemies() {
10  enemiesMoving = true;
11  yield return new WaitForSeconds(turnDelay);
12  if (enemies.Count == 0) {
13    yield return new WaitForSeconds(turnDelay);
14  }
15  List<Enemy> enemiesToDestroy = new List<Enemy>();
16  for (int i = 0; i < enemies.Count; i++) {
17    if (playerInDungeon) {
18      if ((!enemies[i].getSpriteRenderer().isVisible)) {
19        if (i == enemies.Count - 1)
20          yield return new WaitForSeconds(enemies[i].moveTime);
21        continue;
22      }
23    } else {
24      if ((!enemies[i].getSpriteRenderer().isVisible) ||
          (!boardScript.checkValidTile
          (enemies[i].transform.position))) {
25        enemiesToDestroy.Add(enemies[i]);
26        continue;
27      }
28    }
...
29 public void enterDungeon () {
30   dungeonScript.StartDungeon ();
31   boardScript.SetDungeonBoard (dungeonScript.gridPositions,
       dungeonScript.maxBound, dungeonScript.endPos);
32   playerScript.dungeonTransition = false;
33   playerInDungeon = true;
34
35   for (int i = 0; i < enemies.Count; i++) {
```

```
36     Destroy(enemies[i].gameObject);
37   }
38  enemies.Clear ();
39 }
40
41 public void exitDungeon () {
42   boardScript.SetWorldBoard ();
43   playerScript.dungeonTransition = false;
44   playerInDungeon = false;
45   enemies.Clear ();
46 }
```

Let's jump right in to what's happening in *Code Snip 7.6*:

- `Line 1`: We are adding a `bool` variable to flag when the player is in a dungeon. We are going to need this to determine whether we want to stop the movement of offscreen enemies and destroy them, removing them from the game

- `Line 6`: Inside the `InitGame` function, we are going to set the `playerInDungeon` variable initially to `false`, since we always start on the world board.

- `Lines 17-23`: In the `MoveEnemies` function, we are going to create a conditional statement that if `playerInDungeon` is true, then we want to simply halt the enemy movement until they are back on screen. Otherwise, we add them to the destroy list.

- `Lines 19-20`: This nested condition is important. If we are in the dungeon and all of the enemies are off screen (when we first enter, this will most likely be the case) we need to add a time delay. This condition will cause a time delay on the very last enemy to go through the check. If this condition wasn't present, we would see the player moving too fast and taking half steps that cause a recalculation and jitter effect.

- `Line 33`: During the `enterDungeon` function is when we will set the `playerInDungeon` to `true`.

- `Lines 35-38`: When we enter a dungeon, we'll want to clear all the enemies from the world board.

- `Line 40`: During the `exitDungeon` function is when we will set the `playerInDungeon` to `false`.

- `Line 45`: Since the Dungeon Board is completely destroyed upon exiting, all we need to do to clean up the enemies is clear the list.

And now we have enemies spawning on the Dungeon Board as well. We can give this a quick test by playing the game and entering a dungeon. You should check whether you can move far enough away from an enemy to place it off screen and discontinue its movement. You can then move back and see that the enemy remained in place.

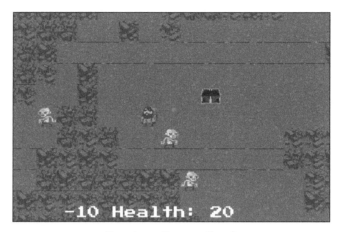

Enemies on Dungeon Board

There are now plenty of enemies in our game to challenge the player. However, at the moment, the player can only flee. We made awesome modular weapons in the previous chapter for this very reason, so it's time to put them to work.

# Fighting the enemy

For this feature, we will need to modify the way the player interacts with his environment one last time. We initially implemented the player `Update` function to interact with only wall tiles. We then needed the player to interact with chest tiles so we forced our `AttemptMove` function to take a wall type on the world board and a chest type on the Dungeon Board. We have yet another tile type that the player can interact with.

We will need to devise a new system that will extract the type of tile the player is interacting with and call `AttemptMove` correctly. This won't be too difficult though. The changes we need to make will take place in the `Player.cs` script, so open that up for editing. Then, take a look at *Code Snip 7.8* to see what has changed:

```
1 private void Update () {
2   if(!GameManager.instance.playersTurn) return;
3   int horizontal = 0;
4   int vertical = 0;
```

```
5    bool canMove = false;
6    horizontal = (int) (Input.GetAxisRaw ("Horizontal"));
7    vertical = (int) (Input.GetAxisRaw ("Vertical"));
8
9    if(horizontal != 0) {
10     vertical = 0;
11   }
12
13   if(horizontal != 0 || vertical != 0) {
14     if (!dungeonTransition) {
15       Vector2 start = transform.position;
16       Vector2 end = start + new Vector2 (horizontal, vertical);
17       base.boxCollider.enabled = false;
18       RaycastHit2D hit = Physics2D.Linecast (start, end,
         base.blockingLayer);
19       base.boxCollider.enabled = true;
20       if (hit.transform != null) {
21         switch(hit.transform.gameObject.tag) {
22         case "Wall":
23           canMove = AttemptMove<Wall> (horizontal, vertical);
24           break;
25         case "Chest":
26           canMove = AttemptMove<Chest> (horizontal, vertical);
27           break;
28         case "Enemy":
29           canMove = AttemptMove<Enemy> (horizontal, vertical);
30           break;
31         }
32       } else {
33         canMove = AttemptMove<Wall> (horizontal, vertical);
34       }
...
35
36 protected override void OnCantMove <T> (T component) {
37   if (typeof(T) == typeof(Wall)) {
38     Wall blockingObj = component as Wall;
39     blockingObj.DamageWall (wallDamage);
40   }
41   else if (typeof(T) == typeof(Chest)) {
42    Chest blockingObj = component as Chest;
43    blockingObj.Open ();
44   }
45   else if (typeof(T) == typeof(Enemy)) {
46     Enemy blockingObj = component as Enemy;
```

```
47      blockingObj.DamageEnemy (wallDamage);
48    }
49
50  animator.SetTrigger ("playerChop");
51
52  if (weapon) {
53    weapon.useWeapon ();
54  }
55 }
```

We first handle when we call `AttemptMove` in the `Update` function. We need to be able to figure out which tile is blocking us and whether we can attack it. Then, we update the `OnCantMove` function and add what happens when we hit an enemy. Let's take a look at the details:

- `Lines 1-34`: This is our `update` function though it is only partial.

- `Lines 15-31`: Here is the new functionality we need to call `AttemptMove` correctly.

- `Lines 15-19`: This is a redundant implementation that mimics what happens in the `MovingObject` class. We need to know what is in front of the player at this point so that we can give `AttempMove` the correct tile type. If there is an object in front of the player, `RaycastHit2D` will return it into hit.

- `Lines 20-31`: If there is an object in hit, we want to enter a switch that will look at the tag of the object and make the corresponding `AttemptMove` call.

- `Lines 45-48`: Lastly, inside the `OnCantMove` function, we add a condition that when the player hits an enemy, we cause damage to that enemy.

Finally, we have added the enemy component to the game. In PCG fashion, the enemies randomly spawn and the player can flee or fight them. Now is a good time for you to take a play test. Try getting as far as you can and remember that if your health drops to 0, the game will end.

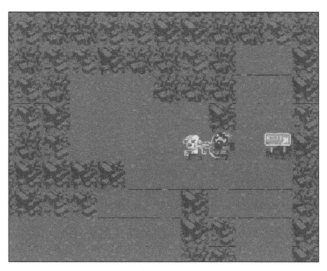
Attacking an enemy

We are not done yet. We want to use PCG to shift the difficulty of the game. We can easily make the enemies that are generated hit harder and take more damage, but that won't change how the player plays the game. It would be more interesting for the player if we were able to create a new environment to adapt to.

# Adaptive difficulty

Adaptive difficulty can be a content generation solution by having enemies carry improved equipment or changing enemy properties such as color and textures. It can also be an Artificial Intelligence question. This is similar to choosing the hard mode at the beginning of a game except, you, the game creator, determine when to engage the hard mode based on some gameplay aspect.

We have already done things such as swapping sprites and changing colors based on strength, so we will be exploring the AI route. We will determine what it takes to adapt the difficulty to the player by changing the AI of the enemy. Eventually, the player will become so strong that one hit from the player will destroy an enemy. So, we want the enemies to be capable of overwhelming the player by getting to the player faster, more efficiently, and in greater numbers.

In order to do this, we will need to adjust the AI capabilities in the `Enemy` class. But first, we will set-up the flags that will determine when and how the difficulty advances. We will start in the `GameManager.cs` script. Add the following variables in *Code Snip 7.9*:

```
1 public bool enemiesFaster = false;
2 public bool enemiesSmarter = false;
3 public int enemySpawnRatio = 20;
```

The variables in *Code Snip 7.9* signify the various advances in difficulty. `enemiesFaster` will trigger enemies to no longer skip a turn. `enemiesSmarter` will trigger the use of a more efficient enemy pathfinding algorithm. `enemySpawnRatio` will make it so enemies appear at a higher frequency.

We need to implement the actual trigger events for these flags now. Every difficulty advancement event is triggered by the player getting stronger. So, we will be placing the event handlers in the `Player.cs` script. *Code Snip 7.10* shows the changes needed to run the adaptive difficulty events:

```
1 private void AdaptDifficulty () {
2   if (wallDamage >= 10)
3     GameManager.instance.enemiesSmarter = true;
4   if (wallDamage >= 15)
5     GameManager.instance.enemiesFaster = true;
6   if (wallDamage >= 20)
7     GameManager.instance.enemySpawnRatio = 10;
8 }
9
10 private void OnTriggerEnter2D (Collider2D other) {
11   if (other.tag == "Exit") {
12     dungeonTransition = true;
13     Invoke ("GoDungeonPortal", 0.5f);
14     Destroy (other.gameObject);
15   } else if (other.tag == "Food" || other.tag == "Soda") {
16     UpdateHealth(other);
17     Destroy (other.gameObject);
18   } else if (other.tag == "Item") {
19     UpdateInventory(other);
20     Destroy (other.gameObject);
21     AdaptDifficulty ();
22   } else if (other.tag == "Weapon") {
23     if (weapon) {
24       Destroy(transform.GetChild(0).gameObject);
25     }
```

```
26    other.enabled = false;
27    other.transform.parent = transform;
28    weapon = other.GetComponent<Weapon>();
29    weapon.AquireWeapon();
30    weapon.inPlayerInventory = true;
31    weapon.enableSpriteRender(false);
32    wallDamage = attackMod + 3;
33    weaponComp1.sprite = weapon.getComponentImage(0);
34    weaponComp2.sprite = weapon.getComponentImage(1);
35    weaponComp3.sprite = weapon.getComponentImage(2);
36    AdaptDifficulty ();
37  }
38 }
```

The event handling for adapting the difficulty to the player's strength is pretty straightforward. First, we add a function called `AdaptDifficulty`, which will hold the cases for each difficulty advancement. Then, we add that function call to whenever the player powers up, which for our game is when the player picks up an item or weapon. Let's see how this is done in the code:

- `Lines 1-8`: This is the `AdaptDifficulty` event handler function. We are watching to see the amount of damage the player can deal out. At a damage of 10, the enemies are shifted to a better AI; at 15, the enemies no longer skip a turn; and at 20, the enemies spawn more frequently.

- `Lines 10-38`: The `OnTriggerEnter2D` function is used to handle item and weapon pickups.

- `Line 21`: We add the `AdaptDifficulty` function call on an item pickup because we will be calculating a new player damage here.

- `Line 36`: We also add the `AdaptDifficulty` function call on a weapon pickup because we will be calculating a new player damage here as well.

Finally, we need to implement the actual events including the better AI functionality. To start off, we should discuss how we plan to implement the said better AI. Luckily, the current AI isn't very complex and improving it won't be difficult.

# Enemy AI

The current AI can be viewed in the `Enemy.cs` script under the `MoveEnemy` function. The AI performs a check on the player position. If the enemy is on the same $x$ coordinate as the player, then the enemy will move towards the player in the $y$ direction. Otherwise, the enemy will move towards the player in the $x$ direction.

Diagram of simple enemy movement

This means that the enemy doesn't try to get around walls. The enemy is easily stuck making it fairly easy for the player to flee. This is perfect in the beginning of the game when the player does very little damage. So our objective is to make it harder for the player to flee when the player becomes strong enough to take on enemy encounters.

Enemy stuck on wall

We have an event that will make the enemy move every turn the player moves. This will decrease the opportunity the player has to get an enemy stuck behind a wall. Then, all our improved AI has to do is add some checks that will allow our enemy to navigate around walls. We can also perform some simple pathfinding that will have our enemy seek to close the distance between it and the player.

Let's begin by selecting a more effective move an enemy can make. The player will be some distance away from the enemy on both the $x$ and $y$ axes. Neither the player nor the enemy can move diagonally, so we can calculate the distance between them on the $x$ axis separate from the $y$ axis. Once we know how many spaces we need to move horizontally and vertically to get to the player, we can make an informed decision on which direction we should take.

Player is 1 space away horizontally and 2 away vertically so enemy moves vertically

The path with the greater distance will be the preferred path because we want the enemy to reach the player as fast as he can. After we have chosen a direction, we need to check that the enemy isn't going to hit anything in that direction. So, we'll check the neighbor cell and see what's in the enemy's way. If there's an obstacle, then we will switch to the next best direction.

Enemy going around wall

For simplicity, we'll only go as far as giving the enemy two attempts to pick the best path. As discussed earlier in the book, pathfinding can be a very complex topic on its own. This algorithm alone will make for a much more challenging game already.

Smarter enemy getting stuck on a wall after two attempts of picking the best path

# Finishing up

So, now that we know what we want to accomplish, let's begin the implementation. Open the Enemy.cs script for editing. *Code Snip 7-10* shows the changes needed for our adaptive difficulty:

```
1 protected override bool AttemptMove <T> (int xDir, int yDir) {
2   if(skipMove && !GameManager.instance.enemiesFaster){
3     skipMove = false;
4     return false;
5   }
6   base.AttemptMove <T> (xDir, yDir);
7
8   skipMove = true;
9   return true;
10 }
11
12 public void MoveEnemy () {
13   int xDir = 0;
14   int yDir = 0;
15
16   if (GameManager.instance.enemiesSmarter) {
17     int xHeading = (int)target.position.x -
       (int)transform.position.x;
18     int yHeading = (int)target.position.y -
       (int)transform.position.y;
19     bool moveOnX = false;
20
```

```
21    if (Mathf.Abs(xHeading) >= Mathf.Abs(yHeading)) {
22      moveOnX = true;
23    }
24    for (int attempt = 0; attempt < 2; attempt++) {
25      if (moveOnX == true && xHeading < 0) {
26        xDir = -1; yDir = 0;
27      }
28      else if (moveOnX == true && xHeading > 0) {
29        xDir = 1; yDir = 0;
30      }
31      else if (moveOnX == false && yHeading < 0) {
32        yDir = -1; xDir = 0;
33      }
34      else if (moveOnX == false && yHeading > 0) {
35        yDir = 1; xDir = 0;
36      }
37
38      Vector2 start = transform.position;
39      Vector2 end = start + new Vector2 (xDir, yDir);
40      base.boxCollider.enabled = false;
41      RaycastHit2D hit = Physics2D.Linecast (start, end,
        base.blockingLayer);
42      base.boxCollider.enabled = true;
43
44      if (hit.transform != null) {
45        if (hit.transform.gameObject.tag == "Wall" ||
          hit.transform.gameObject.tag == "Chest") {
46          if (moveOnX == true)
47            moveOnX = false;
48          else
49            moveOnX = true;
50        } else {
51          break;
52        }
53      }
54    }
55
56  } else {
57    if (Mathf.Abs (target.position.x - transform.position.x) <
      float.Epsilon)
58      yDir = target.position.y > transform.position.y ? 1 : -1;
59    else
60.     xDir = target.position.x > transform.position.x ? 1 : -1;
61  }
62  AttemptMove <Player> (xDir, yDir);
63
64 }
```

We'll start by handling the enemy speed-up event. Then, we'll move on to discuss the improved AI event. Let's take a look at the details of the implementation in *Code Snip 7.10*:

- `Line 2`: We are adding a second condition to the move skip of the enemy. We will also be checking whether the `enemyFaster` flag has been set and if so, we do not skip a move.

- `Line 16`: We are going to start things off in the `MoveEnemy` function by checking whether the `enemySmarter` flag has been set. If so, we will move into our better pathfinding algorithm for our `Enemy` class.

- `Lines 17-18`: We'll calculate the distance from the player to the enemy on the *x* and *y* axis . This can be a negative value, which will tell us if we need to move left (negative x) or down (negative y). A positive value is right (positive x) or up (positive y).

- `Line 19`: The `moveOnX` bool variable will tell us if we need to move horizontal (true) or vertical (false).

- `Lines 21-23`: Here, we will check the magnitude of the x and y distances. Remember, we want the enemy to try to take the longer of the two distances to close the gap between the enemy and player.

- `Line 24`: We want to only make two attempts at picking an optimal path, so we set a `for` loop to run the decision-making process a second time, if need be.

- `Lines 25-36`: This block will determine which direction the enemy will move in. The `moveOnX` variable will tell the enemy to move horizontally or not. The `xHeading` and `yHeading` will tell the enemy to move in the positive or negative direction.

- `Lines 38-42`: We then check whether there is a wall in the way of the direction we have chosen to move in. We do this with `RayCastHit2D` in the same manner we have done in the `Player` and `MovingObject` classes.

- `Lines 44-53`: Lastly, we are going to check whether we hit anything by checking the transform of the hit variable. If we did hit something, we need to determine whether it is a wall or chest because otherwise, we hit the player. If we did hit a wall or chest, we are going to switch the `moveOnX` variable to try a different direction of movement. If we didn't hit anything or we hit the player, we break our `for` loop and continue with the rest of the game execution.

We have just a few more changes to make. In order for this algorithm to work properly in the dungeon, we need to set the OuterWall prefabs' tag to **Wall**. We also need to handle the increased frequency of spawning enemy events. This will be done in the `BoardManager.cs` script.

We only need to change one line in the `BoardManager.cs` script. Inside the `addTiles` function, change the line `else if (Random.Range (0,20) == 1)` to `else if (Random.Range (0, GameManager.instance.enemySpawnRatio) == 1)`. This makes the enemy spawn ratio based on the `GameManager` variable that will change as the player gains strength.

With all of that complete, you can test the full adaptive difficulty functionality. You first need to survive long enough to get a weapon and high-level items to trigger the adaptive difficulty. You can use the **Inspector** tab to verify that all the flags have been set and you can visually verify that the algorithms have taken effect.

# Summary

You are just about finished with our PCG 2D *Roguelike* game! In this chapter, we added the component of enemy opposition and made the difficulty scale with the player.

In this chapter, you added enemies to the game that inherited the same base class as the `Player` class. In PCG fashion, you spawned the enemies at random and had to handle destroying the enemies at the appropriate times. You set up monitoring of the player to scale the difficulty. Instead of just upping the hit points or strength of the enemies to scale the difficulty, you made them faster and smarter by developing a more efficient AI.

We did quite a bit in this chapter, but there is a lot more that we can still do to improve the system. You should continue experimenting with adaptive difficulty. See how much you can improve the AI to make smart enemies with better pathfinding and possibly wall breaking like the player. You can also use randomness to determine how smart an enemy is. Then, you can differentiate between the types of enemies by changing the sprite or the color. Also, don't forget that the player has a `Defense` modifier that can be utilized.

The gameplay of our game is relatively complete. It is time to give it some personality with sound. We are going to step into the more conceptual realms of PCG by making music based on randomness and the player's actions. The next chapter will be the completion of our 2D *Roguelike* game.

# 8
# Generating Music

In this chapter, we are finishing up our *Roguelike* game with the final addition of music. There is still plenty of polishing we can do to the game, such as adding stories or quests, other game sounds, and opening/closing screens. However, the extras can be left to you to finish with your newly acquired knowledge of PCG.

Music is one of the more theoretical subjects we can attempt to procedurally generate. We need general knowledge of how to procedurally generate content and we also need knowledge of music theory so that we can construct a coherent melody. Don't worry, though; we will go through the steps that will give us the information that we need to tackle this task. Here's what you will learn in this chapter:

- Simple music theory
- Create an algorithm from a new theory
- Modularizing code when working with a new subject

Those of you who have a background in music might already have the knowledge needed to complete this chapter. However, for those who do not, we will be covering a basic theory of music. We will only be covering enough music theory to complete the chapter, so feel free to do your own research and go more in depth. Now, let's get started with our final *Roguelike* game chapter!

## Concept of music

Music has existed for many years. It's prehistoric to be precise, and has evolved into a very complicated construct. Even though it is complicated and could take you many years of education to master, music can be very formulaic. The fact that we can abstract the idea of music as a formula is what will allow us to make an algorithm to generate it.

# Tempo

The first thing we need to understand is that a song will follow a tempo. The tempo of a song is the speed at which the song progresses. Every sound within the song falls within some range of the tempo by an equal measure. That measure is usually at pace with the tempo, at 1/4th, at 1/8th, or at 1/16th. The tempo as seen in the following figure:

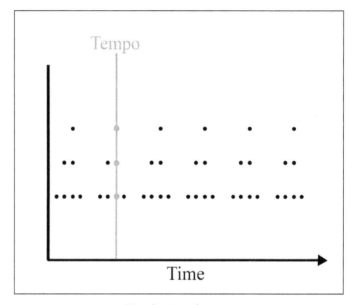

Visualization of tempo

This might sound strange if you have never heard it before. We can visualize each sound following a tempo as dots on a line or in a graph. The tempo can be seen as a vertical line that moves in the positive direction on the $x$ axis. Each time the tempo line intersects a sound dot, the sound will play.

The tempo line moves at a constant rate, but the sound dots can be placed farther apart or closer together. The sound dots are usually placed within the tempo time frame in a uniform distribution. Having your sounds play uniformly with a tempo creates a harmony to your song.

We can think of the tempo as a simple timer. Timers are widely used in game development, so if you haven't been exposed to them, you will learn about them in this chapter. We can set a timer to count down from a set interval and at the end of the timer's life, we play a sound. This will be the basis of our tempo.

# Melody

In a song, the melody is the placement of sounds usually following a tempo that creates an interesting melodic sound as a whole. We will use our tempo timer to play sounds at certain times to create our melody. However, it won't be enough to simply play a sound on a timer.

We will need to vary exactly when and for how long the sound is played within the tempo to make a more interesting melody. Playing sounds at random within the tempo won't work well, as we'll find out later in the chapter with our first attempt at generating music. In order to create a melody that isn't so dissonant that it disturbs the player, we need to play our sounds at equal measures of the tempo.

In the following figure, we see a coordinate plane where the x-axis is time. Our tempo moves along the $x$ axis as time increases. When the tempo intersects with a plotted sound dot, that sound will play. All of the dots are plotted on the $x$ axis, but we vary the $y$ coordinate so that it is easier to read as sounds will sometimes overlap.

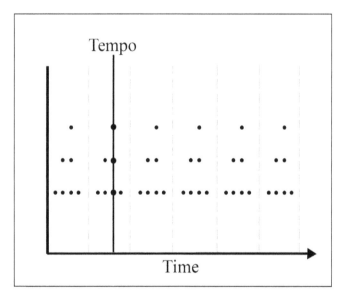

Visualization of tempo divisions

This is where the idea of playing sounds at 1/4th, 1/8th, and 1/16th of the tempo comes in. We will equally space out our sounds at some division of the tempo timer to keep our melody harmonious. But then, we need to consider the sounds that we are playing as well.

We will need a variety of sounds to make our song, as we need a variety of art assets to make a game. Also, in PCG we want to reuse as much as we can, like we did with art, so that we can make the most out of a small amount of sounds. Luckily, there are some simple ways to get the most out of a few sounds.

First, we can vary the length of time for which the sound is played, as shown in the following figure. We will be using some sounds that can be sustained for long periods or played at short intervals. Second, we will be varying the pitch that will change the note at which the sound is played. This will raise and lower the tone of the sound, which is generally used in music to make interesting melodies.

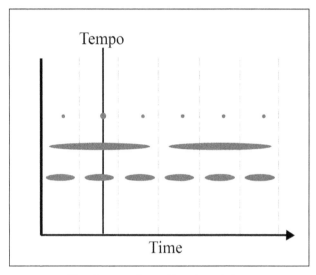

Visualization of sound length variations

# Repetition

Most music follows some sort of repetition. Usually, the song will repeat sections of the song in a pattern, such as VCVC. The V represents a verse where the music will vary in structure and the C represents a chorus where the music structure is consistent. We will simply use the idea of repetition as an excuse to repeat our simple melody.

We will construct a single section of music, such as a verse, and loop it. This will make the song, as a whole, less interesting but this is the desired effect. With the single verse of the song repeating, the tone of the song will become more atmospheric and blend into the background. This way, the player isn't overly distracted by the music in the game.

So now that we know the basics of tempo, melody, and repetition, we are ready to put together a simple song. Since we are generating our song procedurally, we will need to plan out an algorithm, as we have done before. Keep in mind that this will be a small subset of what it can be.

 A great example of a more complex procedural music generator can be experienced at `http://abundant-music.com/`. You can play around with this tool and get inspired to make some procedurally generated music.

## Procedurally generated music algorithm

The design of our algorithm will start with the tempo. As stated before, we can abstract a simple timer into our tempo concept. So we will set a timer at a random interval. When the timer hits 0, then we will play our sound and reset the timer.

This seems simple enough but there is something to consider, the play length of the sound. We are going to vary the play lengths of our sounds, so we need to keep a track of when and for how long the sound will play. We can easily throw off our timer, and as a result, have some sounds playing at different times when the song loops.

## Measure

We can imagine the whole song fitting in a single structure that we will call a **measure**. The measure is the entire time frame of the song before it loops. In order to keep the tempo, we will divide the measure time frame into subsections where our sounds will play.

The following image is a visualization of our measure. There are three horizontal sections that represent the separate sounds that will play in their own time frame. The tempo will move from left to right as the time increases from zero to **t** (how ever long we like).

Visualization of the measure with sounds

By confining our sounds to a constant time frame, we will increase the harmony of the overall song. We don't need the song to be too harmonious as it is meant to be atmospheric and a little creepy. However, the measure will ensure our song doesn't lose timing and transform itself overtime, which may be a little jarring for the player.

## Dividing the measure

For simplicity's sake, our song will consist of three distinct sounds. Feel free to add more sounds, if you like. The measure will be divided uniquely for each sound. We will do a little math to divide the measure so that the sound frequency and play time fits correctly.

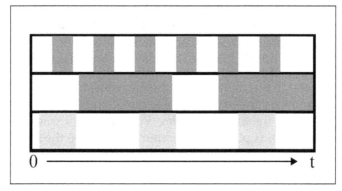

Measure with sound division

We can choose at random how many times the sound is played in the measure. Then, we will need to determine the play length of the sound instances. We can let the sounds play at random lengths within a subdivision of the measure. If we divide the measure by the number of times the sound is played, then we can allow the sound to play no longer than that division.

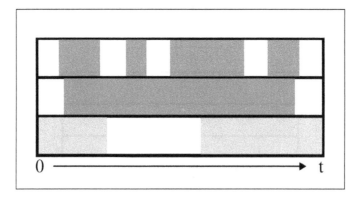

Measure with random sound lengths

The space in between (the white space in the preceding figure) the sound play length is then added together and divided equally. This division will create uniform periods in which the sound is not being played. All of this will ensure that the sound line fits well within the measure and utilizes the space appropriately.

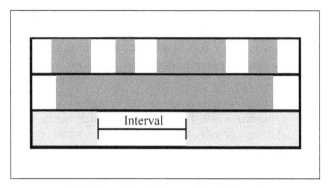

The interval in which sound is not played

Within a single measure, we can add multiple lines of sound that are divided individually to fit the measure. The layering of different sounds following our timer tempo and playing within the same measure will create our song. We can then easily manipulate the pitch each time the sound is played to create a variation in the sound.

So, at this point, our algorithm is pretty well defined. We now need to translate it to code. We can start with a single sound and work our way through it from there.

# The base line

The base line will be our naturally low-pitched sound. We will create this line of bass sounds within a measure division using a single bass sound. But first, we need to set up our script, which will be our `SoundManager` script.

## Setting up the script

Let's first set up the GameObject that will manage the sounds that will make up our game music. We are going to make a `SoundManager` class that is a lot like our `GameManager` class. You can make the Sound Manager using the following steps:

1. Create a new empty GameObject.
2. Name the new GameObject `Sound Manager`.
3. Add three audio source components to the `Sound Manager` GameObject.

After you have the `Sound Manager` GameObject, we will need to import some sounds. You can find the three main sounds we will use for this chapter in the accompanying files under `Chapter 8`. Create a new folder called `Sounds` and import `sound1.wav`, `sound2.wav`, and `sound3.wav` into the `Sounds` folder.

Then, return to the `Sound Manager` GameObject and add each sound to the **Audio Clip** section of the three audio sources. That is all we need to do right now for the `Sound Manager` setup. It is important to note that two of the three sounds that we are using have a particular quality to them.

 All three sounds were created using an online synthesizer called **AudioSauna**, which can be found at `http://www.audiosauna.com/studio/`.

Both `sound1.wav` and `sound2.wav` were recorded for a longer time frame (about 7 seconds) because the sounds' wave form can be infinite. That means, we can play these sounds at a constant rate for some time as opposed to `sound3.wav`, which will dampen on its own after some time.

## The Sound Manager script

Now that we are all set up, we are ready to write the script. Create a `SoundManager.cs` script in the **Scripts** folder. Then, open the script for editing. *Code Snip 8.1* shows our new `SoundManager` class. As a warning, the following code snippet is not our final product and we will be improving it throughout the chapter:

```
1 using UnityEngine;
2 using System;
3 using System.Collections;
4 using Random = UnityEngine.Random;
5
6 public class SoundManager : MonoBehaviour {
7
8   public static SoundManager instance = null;
9
10  public AudioSource highSource;
11  public AudioSource midSource;
12  public AudioSource lowSource;
13
14  public float lowPitchRange = 0.0f;
15  public float highPitchRange = 0.0f;
16
17  public float measure = 0.0f;
```

```
18
19  public float[] basePlayTime;
20  public float basePlayTimer = 0.0f;
21  public float baseInterval = 0.0f;
22  public float baseIntervalTimer = 0.0f;
23  public int baseCords;
24  private float[] basePitchRanges;
25  public int basePitchRangeCount = 0;
26
27  void Awake() {
28    if (instance == null)
29      instance = this;
30    else if (instance != this)
31      Destroy(gameObject);
32
33    DontDestroyOnLoad(gameObject);
34
35    lowPitchRange = 0.25f;
36    highPitchRange = 1.75f;
37
38    Init();
39  }
40
41  void Update() {
42
43    PlaySoundLine(lowSource,
44      basePlayTime,
45      ref basePlayTimer,
46      baseInterval,
47      ref baseIntervalTimer,
48      baseCords,
49      basePitchRanges,
50      ref basePitchRangeCount);
51  }
52
53  private void Init() {
54
55    measure = Random.Range(3.0f, 20.0f);
56    float playTotal = 0.0f;
57
58    baseCords = Random.Range(3, 7);
59    basePlayTime = new float[baseCords];
60    basePitchRanges = new float[baseCords];
61    for (int i = 0; i < baseCords; i++)
```

```
62   {
63     basePlayTime[i] = Random.Range(3.0f / baseCords, measure /
       baseCords);
64     playTotal += basePlayTime[i];
65     basePitchRanges[i] = Random.Range(lowPitchRange,
       highPitchRange);
66   }
67   basePlayTimer = basePlayTime[0];
68
69   baseInterval = (measure - playTotal) / baseCords;
70   baseIntervalTimer = baseInterval;
71 }
72
73 private void PlaySoundLine(AudioSource audio,
74   float[] playTime,
75   ref float playTimer,
76   float interval,
77   ref float intervalTimer,
78   int cords,
79   float[] pitchRanges,
80   ref int pitchRangeCount)
81   {
82     if (pitchRangeCount >= cords)
83     {
84       pitchRangeCount = 0;
85     }
86
87     if (playTimer > 0)
88     {
89       playTimer -= Time.deltaTime;
90       if (!audio.isPlaying)
91       {
92         audio.pitch = pitchRanges[pitchRangeCount];
93         audio.Play();
94         pitchRangeCount++;
95       }
96     }
97     else if (playTimer <= 0)
98       {
99         audio.Stop();
100
101         if (intervalTimer > 0)
102         {
103           intervalTimer -= Time.deltaTime;
```

```
104          }
105          else if (intervalTimer <= 0)
106          {
107            playTimer = playTime[pitchRangeCount];
108            intervalTimer = interval;
109          }
110      }
111    }
112 }
```

This is a rather large code block, so we will take a look at it in blocks. First, we will go over our declarations, then the `Awake` function, then we'll jump to the `Init` and `PlaySoundLine`, and finally, return to the `Update` function. So, in that order, let's go over an explanation of the `SoundManager` code:

- `Lines 1-4`: These are our general using directives that you've seen throughout the book.

- `Lines 8-25`: These lines are our variable declarations and there are quite a few of them. We'll give a brief explanation of each one. The `SoundManager` instance — the `SoundManager` class will be a singleton and is set up exactly like the `GameManager` class.

- `Lines 10-12`: Here are our `AudioSource` references. Each sound will be called from an `AudioSource` that we attached to the Sound Manager prefab. We will only be working with the `lowSource` instance for right now.

- `Lines 14-15`: These are the pitch ranges that our sounds can have. We will be dynamically changing these values, so initialize them at 0.

- `Line 17`: This is our measure variable, which will be a single float value representing the time frame in which all the sounds are played.

- `Line 19`: The play times for the `lowSource` instance. We will refer to this as the base line sounds because it will make up the tempo/rhythm for the other sounds to follow. The `basePlayTime` is an array because the sound will play multiple times in a measure and at differing lengths.

- `Line 20`: `basePlayTimer` is the play timer. We will need a variable dedicated to timing the play length of the current `lowSource` sound. We will have several variables like this.

- `Line 21`: `baseInterval` is the internal time frame. The interval is the amount of time between the sound playing. Remember from the algorithm design that we are going to use this value to calculate the other values.

- `Line 22`: `baseIntervalTimer` is another dedicated timer. This one is for timing the interval or wait period between sound plays.

- Line 23: baseCords is the number of times the sound will play within a measure. This number will be the length of the basePlayTimes and basePitchRanges arrays.

- Line 24: basePitchRanges is the array that holds the pitch range values that correlate to the basePlayTimes array.

- Line 25: Finally, we'll use pitchRangeCount to keep track of which pitch value we need to attach to the sound.

- Lines 27-39: After all those variable declarations, we are at the Awake function. Here, we will set up the SoundManager class to be a singleton, just like we do in the GameManager class. Then, we set our initial values for our pitch range and call the Init function, which will calculate our sounds within our measure.

- Lines 53-71: The Init function is where we will decide the length of our measure and calculate how the sound will be played within that measure. First, we randomly decide the length of the measure, and then, we declare a helper variable that will track how much time in total of the measure is spent playing the sound.

- Lines 58-60: We randomly decide the number of times we play the sound as baseCords. We then use that number to initialize our basePlayTimes and basePitchRanges arrays.

- Lines 61-66: When calculating the basePlayTimes, we do a little math. We are going to let the basePlayTimes array be decided at random, but we can't let them be too long or it will mess up our measure timing. So the minimum of our range dictates that the sound can play for no less than the minimum length of a measure divided by the number of times we want to play the sound. Likewise, the sound can play for no longer than the full length of our measure divided by the number of sound plays. This will restrict the sound to play in intervals that are well contained within the measure. Then, we add this calculated play time to the total of playTotal and randomize the pitch for that sound to play.

- Line 67: We want to initialize the basePlayTimer array to hold the first play time.

- Lines 69-70: Lastly, we will calculate the baseInterval array to be an even distribution of the leftover time that the sound is not playing. The way we do this is we subtract the total play time from the total measure time and divide it by the number of times the sound is played.

- Lines `73-112`: Moving on to the `PlaySoundLine` function, this is where the `AudioSource` method will be called and the play timers will be run. We pass into the function all the variables we track for the `lowSource` sound. Some of the variables, mainly the timers, are passed as `ref`, which means their values will be globally updated in the script.

- Lines `82-85`: This is a check that resets the `pitchRangeCount` variable. The `pitchRangeCount` variable will increase over time representing which pitch is being applied to the sound.

- Lines `87-96`: This first check is to see if our `playTimer` is running. If the timer hasn't hit zero yet, we want to decrease the time. Then, we check if the sound is playing. If not, we play it with the selected pitch and adjust the `pitchRangeCount` for next time. We check to see if the sound is playing we can then skip playing the song so that we don't start it from the beginning.

- Lines `97-111`: If the `playTimer` variable hits 0, then we stop the sound. We will also start the interval wait period. After the `intervalTimer` variable hits 0, we set the `playTime` value to match the `pitchRangeCount` value, which was adjusted during the playing of the sound. We are using `pitchRangeCount` as the dynamic value and cords as the constant to reset.

- Lines `41-51`: Lastly, the `Update` function calls the `PlaySoundLine` function. The `Update` function is called once per frame, which happens many times within a second of the game and is ideal for use of timing.

And after all that, you can add this script to the Sound Manager prefab. You will need to add the three Audio Sources in our Sound Manager component to their source locations in the `SoundManager` script. Then, go ahead and play the game. You should hear a low bass sound. Try stopping and starting the game several times to hear how it changes.

That was quite a bit to get through, but we're not done yet. It's not much of a song to only have one sound playing. So, next, we are going to add our two other sounds. But we need to be aware of good coding practices.

As of right now, we can easily add the sounds to our script, but it will make for some unappealing code. We are tracking a large number of variables for our base sound and we would have to add those same variables per new sound. Take a look at *Code Snip 8.2* to see an example:

```
1   public float basePlayTime = 0.0f;
2   public float basePlayTimer = 0.0f;
3 public float baseInterval = 0.0f;
4   public float baseIntervalTimer = 0.0f;
5   public int baseCords;
```

```
 6  private float[] basePitchRanges;
 7  public int basePitchRangeCount = 0;
 8
 9  public float midPlayTime = 0.0f;
10  public float midPlayTimer = 0.0f;
11  public float midInterval = 0.0f;
12  public float midIntervalTimer = 0.0f;
13  public int midCords;
14  private float[] midPitchRanges;
15  public int midPitchRangeCount = 0;
16
17  public float highPlayTime = 0.0f;
18  public float highPlayTimer = 0.0f;
19  public float highInterval = 0.0f;
20  public float highIntervalTimer = 0.0f;
21  public int highCords;
22  private float[] highPitchRanges;
23  public int highPitchRangeCount = 0;
24
25  void Update () {
26    PlaySoundLine (lowSource,
27      basePlayTime,
28      ref basePlayTimer,
29      baseInterval,
30      ref baseIntervalTimer,
31      baseCords,
32      basePitchRanges,
33      ref basePitchRangeCount);
34
35    PlaySoundLine (midSource,
36      midPlayTime,
37      ref midPlayTimer,
38      midInterval,
39      ref midIntervalTimer,
40      midCords,
41      midPitchRanges,
42      ref midPitchRangeCount);
43
44    PlaySoundLine (highSource,
45      highPlayTime,
46      ref highPlayTimer,
47      highInterval,
48      ref highIntervalTimer,
49      highCords,
```

```
50    highPitchRanges,
51    ref highPitchRangeCount);
52
53 }
```

As you can see, we would have to heavily repeat ourselves in the code and it would quickly become an unnecessarily large file. Instead, what we can do is make things a little more modular. By adding a class that would encapsulate the sound variables, the sound calculations, and the playing of the sound, we can make it so that adding a new sound would only require a few new lines. This would make our script scale better as we could also devise a system to dynamically add sounds.

All that we need to do is declare a class within the Sound Manager, and then copy our functionality into that new class. Then, we can slightly rewrite our functions to call the class methods instead. Check out *Code Snip 8.3* to see how this is done:

```
1 public class SoundManager : MonoBehaviour {
2
3   [Serializable]
4   public class AudioCtrl
5   {
6     public float[] pitchRanges;
7     public float[] playTimes;
8     public float playTimer;
9     public float interval;
10    public float intervalTimer;
11    public int cordCount;
12    public int rangeCount;
13
14    public AudioCtrl () {
15      playTimer = 0.0f;
16      interval = 0.0f;
17      intervalTimer = 0.0f;
18      cordCount = 0;
19      rangeCount = 0;
20    }
21
22    public void CalculateAudio (float measure, int minFreq, int
      maxFreq, float low, float high) {
23      float playTotal = 0.0f;
24
25      cordCount = Random.Range (minFreq, maxFreq);
26      playTimes = new float[cordCount];
27      pitchRanges = new float[cordCount];
```

```
28      for (int i = 0; i < cordCount; i++) {
29        playTimes[i] = Random.Range (minFreq/cordCount,
          measure/cordCount);
30        playTotal += playTimes[i];
31        pitchRanges[i] = Random.Range(low, high);
32      }
33      playTimer = playTimes[0];
34
35      interval = (measure - playTotal) / cordCount;
36      intervalTimer = interval;
37    }
38
39    public void PlaySoundLine (AudioSource source) {
40
41      if (rangeCount >= cordCount) {
42        rangeCount = 0;
43      }
44
45      if (playTimer > 0){
46        playTimer -= Time.deltaTime;
47        if (!source.isPlaying) {
48          source.pitch = pitchRanges[rangeCount];
49          source.Play();
50          rangeCount++;
51        }
52      }
53      else if (playTimer <= 0){
54        source.Stop();
55
56        if (intervalTimer > 0){
57          intervalTimer -= Time.deltaTime;
58        }
59        else if (intervalTimer <= 0){
60          playTimer = playTimes[rangeCount];
61          intervalTimer = interval;
62        }
63      }
64    }
65  }
66
67  public static SoundManager instance = null;
68
69  public AudioSource highSource;
70  public AudioSource midSource;
```

```
71  public AudioSource lowSource;
72
73  public float lowPitchRange = 0.0f;
74  public float highPitchRange = 0.0f;
75
76  public float measure = 0.0f;
77
78  public AudioCtrl baseAudio;
79  public AudioCtrl midAudio;
80  public AudioCtrl highAudio;
81
82  void Awake () {
83    if (instance == null)
84      instance = this;
85    else if (instance != this)
86      Destroy (gameObject);
87
88    DontDestroyOnLoad (gameObject);
89
90    lowPitchRange = 0.25f;
91    highPitchRange = 1.75f;
92
93    baseAudio = new AudioCtrl ();
94    midAudio = new AudioCtrl ();
95    highAudio = new AudioCtrl ();
96
97    FormAudio ();
98  }
99
100 void Update () {
101   baseAudio.PlaySoundLine (lowSource);
102   midAudio.PlaySoundLine (midSource);
103   highAudio.PlaySoundLine (highSource);
104 }
105
106 public void FormAudio () {
107   measure = Random.Range (1.0f, 20.0f);
108
109   baseAudio.CalculateAudio(measure, 3, 7, lowPitchRange,
      highPitchRange);
110   midAudio.CalculateAudio(measure, 2, 6, lowPitchRange,
      highPitchRange);
111   highAudio.CalculateAudio(measure, 5, 10, lowPitchRange,
      highPitchRange);
112
113 }
114 }
```

This is another large code block, but keep in mind that this is more of a code rearrangement than an addition of functionality. The main task of this is to modularize our sound effects so that we can easily add more sounds. So let's take a look at what we've done:

- Lines 3-4: Here is the declaration of our new AudioCtrl helper class. We are also going to serialize the class so that we can see its properties in the Unity Editor.

- Lines 6-12: These lines of the AudioCtrl class are the variables we used to manage our base sound. We have renamed them slightly because these properties are now universal to any AudioCtrl sound.

- Lines 14-20: This is the AudioCtrl constructor. It simply initializes all single values to 0. The arrays will be initialized later in the class.

- Lines 22-36: The CalculateAudio method of the AudioCtrl class will use the sound variables and calculate the play times of the sound based on the measure. This is the Init function from the last version of code.

- Lines 38-63: The PlaySoundLine function is the PlaySoundLine from the last version of code as well. We have made some variable name adjustments to use the AudioCtrl internal properties.

- Lines 67-80: After the AudioCtrl class declaration, we have the regular variable declarations for the SoundManager class. The only difference here is that instead of declaring a group of variables for each sound source, we declare a new AudioCtrl instance.

- Lines 81-97: In the Awake function, we initialize the AudioCtrl instances and call a new function called FormAudio.

- Lines 99-103: Our Update function is still only three function calls, but they are much more compact than the variables have been compartmentalized more efficiently, adding other sounds.

- Lines 105-111: Lastly, our FormAudio function just acts as a driver to call CalculateAudio on each of the AudioCtrl instances. The measure length is also decided here. The numbers in the function calls represent the min and max range of how many times within the measure a sound is played. Feel free to change these numbers to create a sound combination that you enjoy.

So, we cleaned up our code and simultaneously added two more sounds to our song. Now, you can head back to the Unity Editor and give the new setup a test. You might need to reset your Audio Sources in the SoundManager script on the Game Object.

Try stopping and starting the game to generate new songs. You might notice that sometimes the song has a fast pace or a slow pace. The pace or tempo of the song is controlled with the measure range that was set in the `FormAudio` function.

It would be a fun adjustment to our script if we could manipulate the measure during game play and thus change the tempo of the music as we play. Usually, you have atmospheric music as you explore in a game and then the music gets tenser and the tempo increases when you are in a battle or in a similar situation. We are going to add the functionality to change the tempo on our song, depending on what we are doing in the game. We can also make an adjustment to increase the melodic nature of our song.

# Adding tension

This addition will need to take place in the `GameManager` class as well, but we will start in the `SoundManager` class. First, we will try to add some more melody to our song. There is a rise and fall nature to music. The sound will rise in pitch and then lower creating a rhythm.

We will add in some pitch control to attempt a similar effect. This change will take place in the `CalculateAudio` function of the `SoundManager` class. Take a look at *Code Snip 8.4* to see the changes:

```
1 public void CalculateAudio (float measure, int minFreq, int
  maxFreq, float low, float high) {
2    float playTotal = 0.0f;
3    float lastPitch = Random.Range(low, high);
4    int switchPitchCount = Random.Range(3, maxFreq);
5    int switchPitch = 0;
6    int pitchDir = Random.Range(0, 2);
7
8    cordCount = Random.Range (minFreq, maxFreq);
9    playTimes = new float[cordCount];
10   pitchRanges = new float[cordCount];
11   for (int i = 0; i < cordCount; i++) {
12     playTimes[i] = Random.Range (minFreq/cordCount,
       measure/cordCount);
13     playTotal += playTimes[i];
14     if (pitchDir == 0) {
15       lastPitch = pitchRanges[i] = Random.Range(low, lastPitch);
16     }
17     else if (pitchDir == 1) {
18       lastPitch = pitchRanges[i] = Random.Range(lastPitch,
         high);
```

```
19    }
20    switchPitch++;
21    if (switchPitch == switchPitchCount) {
22      if (pitchDir == 0)
23        pitchDir = 1;
24      else
25        pitchDir = 0;
26    }
27  }
28  playTimer = playTimes[0];
29
30  interval = (measure - playTotal) / cordCount;
31  intervalTimer = interval;
32 }
```

We added some new local variables that will keep track of the pitch. Then, we added some checks that will dictate whether we want to adjust the pitch lower or higher. Let's go through the code:

- `Line 3:` `lastPitch` will be the current pitch value.

- `Line 4:` `switchPitchCount` will be the number of times the pitch value changes.

- `Line 5:` `switchPitch` will be a flag to indicate that we are switching whether a pitch should increase or decrease.

- `Line 6:` `pitchDir` is the indicator that the pitch is increasing or decreasing. 1 for increasing and 0 for decreasing.

- `Lines 14-19:` We will calculate the pitch of the sound with the play time calculation. First, we check to see in which direction the pitch needs to go. If 0, we want the pitch to stay the same or to go lower. If 1, we want the pitch to stay the same or to go higher.

- `Lines 19-26:` After we choose a pitch or a sound play, we add to the countdown of the pitch's direction change. If it's time to change the pitch's direction, then we adjust `pitchDir` accordingly.

So that quick change should give our music a bit more melody. Use this and adjust the frequency values in the `PlaySoundLine` calls to create a general sound that you like. Now, we will move on to adjusting the measure during game play.

Still in the `SoundManager` class , you'll make a small change. In the `FormAudio` function, you'll add a check for a flag. We can then call `FormAudio` from the `GameManager` with the flag active or not to change the tempo.

The flag, which we will call tension, will be set when you encounter enemies. In FormAudio, we'll simply adjust the range in which the measure can choose from. You can see this in *Code Snip 8.5*:

```
1 public void FormAudio (bool tension) {
2
3   if (tension) {
4     measure = Random.Range (1.0f, 3.0f);
5   } else {
6     measure = Random.Range (10.0f, 20.0f);
7   }
8
9   baseAudio.CalculateAudio(measure, 3, 7, lowPitchRange,
    highPitchRange);
10  midAudio.CalculateAudio(measure, 2, 6, lowPitchRange,
    highPitchRange);
11  highAudio.CalculateAudio(measure, 5, 10, lowPitchRange,
    highPitchRange);
12
13 }
```

Lines 3-7 show the check that is needed. If the tension flag is set, measure will choose from a lower range of measure time frames, which will increase the frequency of sound plays. This, thus, increases the tempo and the anxiety of the song.

We need to also change how we call the function and where. Starting in the Awake function of the SoundManager class, change the FormAudio call to FormAudio(false). Then, we'll need to open up the GameManager script to add some FormAudio calls. The changes to the GameManager class can be seen in *Code Snip 8.6*:

```
14 public void AddEnemyToList(Enemy script)
15 {
16   enemies.Add(script);
17   SoundManager.instance.FormAudio (true);
18 }
19 public void RemoveEnemyFromList(Enemy script)
20 {
21   enemies.Remove(script);
22   if (enemies.Count == 0) {
23     SoundManager.instance.FormAudio (false);
24   }
25 }
...
26 public void exitDungeon () {
27   boardScript.SetWorldBoard ();
```

```
28     playerScript.dungeonTransition = false;
29     playerInDungeon = false;
30     enemies.Clear ();
31
32     SoundManager.instance.FormAudio (false);
33 }
```

The adjustment is minor but will make a good impact on game play. Simply add the `SoundManager.instance.FormAudio` call to the `AddEnemyToList`, `RemoveEnemyFromList`, and `exitDungeon` functions. You will need to add a check to the `RemoveEnemyFromList` function that checks whether all enemies have been removed.

Now, when you play the game, the tempo of our song will play slower and more melodic. Find an enemy and the tempo of the song will increase, which will make it feel as though there is some tension. This all adds to the overall fun of the game.

# Summary

That completes our chapter building and our PCG *Roguelike* game. The game is by no means done, but it is very much playable. This is a great starter project that you can, and should, finish on you own. Every piece of this project was done using the theory of PCG, but it all can be improved.

For example, the music in this chapter can easily use more sounds. You can even add to the Sound Manager, making it choose 5-10 sounds from a large list of preloaded sounds. Use your imagination and continue building with PCG.

You learned some simple music theory. You learned how to approach changing a complex subject into an algorithm. And lastly, you took some time and modularized your code to make it neater and more reusable.

Remember, PCG doesn't stop at visual art or music. Be inventive when you approach PCG. You can procedurally generate anything. Think about how you can procedurally generate story, AI behavior, sounds, user interfaces, animations, or anything really!

We are done with our 2D *Roguelike* game for now, but we have one more subject left to discuss. We are going to take a brief view of PCG in 3D space. In the next chapter, we will build a planet generator and explore some PCG worlds.

# Generating a 3D Planet

So far we've tackled 2D content generation and some complex sound generation. You made a 2D *Roguelike* game that can continually generate game content for as long as the player can survive. However, with our 2D game complete, it's time to add another dimension to our PCG learning and move into 3D.

In this chapter, we will be procedurally generating a 3D planet. You can see an example of a procedurally generated shape in the following figure. Then, just for fun, we'll add the scripts necessary to take a first person view walk on that planet. However, 3D does pose some new considerations when applying PCG. Here's what you can expect to learn in this chapter:

- 2D versus 3D rendering
- Space and time complexity of 3D object generation
- 3D geometry considerations with PCG

A procedurally generated sphere

Generating 3D objects is basically graphics programming. Math can be used to describe everything around us in a geometric sense. Then, we take that math and make it an algorithm for drawing points and lines on a graph and rendering it to our screen. Graphics programming is a very interesting and spectacular subfield of computer science, but be prepared to study lots of advanced mathematics to get good at it.

We will be dealing with more math in this chapter than the previous ones. Since graphics programming is a vast subject that has many books already written about it, the explanations of the mathematics will be brief. These are just equations that can be looked up and researched at your leisure. So without further delay, let's start learning some PCG in 3D.

# Adding a third dimension

Unity makes 2D game development very easy. Don't forget that underneath Unity's user interface, there are a lot of calculations being done for us. In many other graphics rendering engines, we would have to write the code that creates the 2D square that we can then draw our sprite on. With Unity, we simply add a component or two. In the following figure, we can see a 2D sprite from a 3D perspective. A sprite is after all just a quad that is rendered facing the camera.

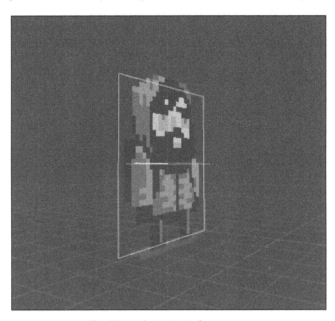

The 2D quad a sprite is drawn onto

Unity also makes 3D game development much easier. Instead of using quads for sprite rendering, in 3D, we will work from 3D models. A 3D model is a collection of vertices, or points, in 3D space. We then connect those dots and make faces or triangles. This comprises the wireframe structure and surface of our model.

For most games, a 3D model is created by a 3D modeling program or software and then imported into Unity. We will then assign appropriate components to the imported model. We can then easily manipulate the 3D models with physics and animation. This is convenient because it can be very difficult and time consuming trying to program an algorithm to create a complex 3D model.

This is exactly what we are going to do though. We are going to bypass the modeling phase and write a script that creates a model for us. We want to do this to introduce that random factor. However, as stated before, this can get very time consuming and complex. There are a few things that change drastically when applying PCG to 3D as opposed to 2D.

# 3D versus 2D

Because 3D objects can become very complex very quickly, we need to keep two things in mind when we write our algorithms: time and space. We need to be aware that certain tasks can take a long time because there is a lot for the computer to process and some tasks can take a lot of space in terms of memory. In computer science, this is the study of **time complexity** and **space complexity**.

We need to understand that creating and managing 3D objects can take a long time because there are a lot of pieces to a 3D object. We need to calculate the position of every point and draw every triangle between those points. This ultimately means longer load times and/or some slowing during gameplay.

Space management also becomes a concern when generating 3D objects. The more complex an object is, the more memory it will need to use in its calculations. Information on every point, triangle, and more needs to be stored somewhere when generating 3D objects. The more 3D objects that are being drawn onscreen, the more memory will be consumed and possibly slow down the gameplay.

Fortunately, graphics programming is a field that is widely researched and developed. There are plenty of references online alone that can aid in generating a wide range of 3D objects. The 3D primitives (cubes, cylinders, spheres, polygons, and so on) all have an equation that has been made into an efficient algorithm already. We just need to keep in mind that there are usually several ways to make a shape and some might suit our needs better than others.

# Know your geometry

In this chapter, we will be working with spheres. Spheres in particular can be represented by quite a few 3D primitives and other polygons. The Unity primitive sphere is actually a cube that has had its vertices interpolated and edges slightly moved to make more of a curve. You can see the corners of the cube in the sphere wireframe:

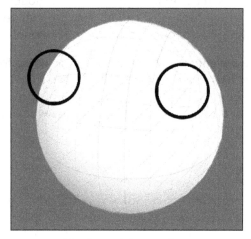

3D cube made into a sphere

# Working with the Unity primitive sphere

There aren't too many uses for the Unity 3D primitive shapes. Their primary use will be in prototypes as a placeholder. Usually, anything that is used in a game has been designed and modeled to a specification. With that said, we are going to start with a Unity primitive just to see how it works and why we might want to use something else instead.

The Unity primitive sphere has a certain property that makes it a little difficult to manipulate. The triangles that make up the sphere are all distinct and separate. Each triangle has its own vertices and where triangles meet, there is a cluster of separate vertices. When we start moving theses vertices, we will split the seams of the model and open it up. Usually, meshes only render on one side of a 3D model. So meshes that open up will appear transparent at the back of the triangles. The effect can be seen in the following figure:

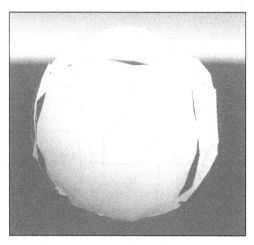

Sphere triangles splitting when moved

To solve this, we will have to add some extra functionality to group the vertices. So, when one vertex moves, all of the vertices in the same position will move to the same new location. Let's try out writing a script to randomize the vertices while not distorting the mesh so much that it renders improperly.

Be sure to set up a new project with a fresh scene in 3D mode. Create a new C# script called MoveVertices and open it up for editing. *Code Snip 9.1* shows the script:

```
1 using UnityEngine;
2 using System;
3 using System.Collections.Generic;
4 using Random = UnityEngine.Random;
5
6 public class MoveVertices : MonoBehaviour {
7
8     Mesh mesh;
9     Vector3[] vertices;
10
11    void Start () {
12        mesh = GetComponent<MeshFilter>().mesh;
13        vertices = mesh.vertices;
14
15        mesh.vertices = Randomize(vertices);
16    }
17
18    Vector3[] Randomize(Vector3[] verts) {
19        Dictionary<Vector3, List<int>> dictionary = new
           Dictionary<Vector3, List<int>>();
```

```
20
21          for (int x = 0; x < verts.Length; x++) {
22              if (!dictionary.ContainsKey(verts[x])) {
23                  dictionary.Add(verts[x], new List<int>());
24              }
25
26              dictionary[verts[x]].Add(x);
27          }
28
29          foreach (KeyValuePair<Vector3, List<int>> pair in
            dictionary) {
30            Vector3 newPos = pair.Key * Random.Range(0.9f, 1.1f);
31              foreach (int i in pair.Value) {
32                  verts[i] = newPos;
33              }
34          }
35
36          return verts;
37      }
38 }
```

After writing the script, you can make a sphere primitive in the editor by navigating to **GameObject** | **3D Object** | **Sphere** from the menu. You can then attach this script to the object and run it to see its effects. The randomization of the vertices makes a sort of bumpiness or terrain on the sphere. Now, let's see what is happening in the code:

- Lines 1-4: These are our general using statements. We use Generic for the dictionary class and set Random to Unity.Random.

- Lines 8-9: We will be working with two members, the sphere's Mesh component and the set of vertices that make up that mesh.

- Lines 11-16: In the Start function, we will set a reference to the Mesh component, grab the array of vertices from that mesh, and call the Randomize function.

- Lines 18-19: The Randomize function takes an array of Vector3 objects. We are going to set up a dictionary to store the location of a vertex as a key and map that to a list of vertices that share the same location.

- Lines 21-27: We want to loop through all the vertices and add their location to our dictionary. If the vertex location hasn't been added yet, then we add it; if it has, then we add that vertex to the list of vertices at that location.

- `Lines 29-34`: Once we have our dictionary of grouped vertices, we will loop through each vertex position. For each vertex position, we want to choose a new random location, loop through every vertex in the current location, and change it to the new location.

Now, our sphere has a bumpy structure to it. You can vary the size of the sphere and the randomization range for different results. Try experimenting with this script and see what you come up with.

The main issue with using the Unity primitive is that you don't get to choose the natural size and how many vertices you want in the mesh. So the better option is to generate our own sphere. However, we have to be aware that this might slow down our system. As with our `MoveVertices` script, we looped through a large set of vertices several times. The number of vertices and loop passes all add up against performance.

# Generating a sphere

As stated before, generating a sphere entails plotting points based on an equation. The equation is geometry-based and made into an algorithm to plot the vertices. Teaching the bases of graphics programming would be a book in itself. Thus, the explanation of the math will be brief.

There happens to be quite a few ways to make a sphere. We can take a simple 3D shape and interpolate or multiply the vertices in a structured fashion, smoothing as we go. There are a lot of algorithms available online and each might make slightly different kinds of spheres.

The algorithm we are going to use can be found at the Unity Wiki page, `http://wiki.unity3d.com/index.php/ProceduralPrimitives`. There are also other 3D primitives on this page that you can generate. The sphere we are going to generate is a polar sphere, which is the common sphere that is generated. So, now create a new C# script called `ProceduralSphere.cs` and open it up for editing. *Code Snip 9.2* shows the script:

```
1 using UnityEngine;
2 using System.Collections;
3 using System.Collections.Generic;
4 using Random = UnityEngine.Random;
5
6 public class ProceduralSphere : MonoBehaviour {
7
8     private Mesh mesh;
9     private MeshFilter filter;
```

```
10
11     void Start () {
12         GenerateSphere(0.5f, 16, 16);
13     }
14
15     private void GenerateSphere (float radius, int nbLong, int
       nbLat) {
16         filter = gameObject.AddComponent<MeshFilter>();
17         mesh = filter.mesh;
18         mesh.Clear();
19
20         #region Vertices
21         Vector3[] vertices = new Vector3[(nbLong + 1) * nbLat +
           2];
22         float _pi = Mathf.PI;
23         float _2pi = _pi * 2f;
24
25         vertices[0] = Vector3.up * radius;
26         for (int lat = 0; lat < nbLat; lat++)
27         {
28             float a1 = _pi * (float)(lat + 1) / (nbLat + 1);
29             float sin1 = Mathf.Sin(a1);
30             float cos1 = Mathf.Cos(a1);
31
32             for (int lon = 0; lon <= nbLong; lon++)
33             {
34                 float a2 = _2pi * (float)(lon == nbLong ? 0 :
                   lon) / nbLong;
35                 float sin2 = Mathf.Sin(a2);
36                 float cos2 = Mathf.Cos(a2);
37
38                 vertices[lon + lat * (nbLong + 1) + 1] = new
                   Vector3(sin1 * cos2, cos1, sin1 * sin2) *
                   radius;
39             }
40         }
41         vertices[vertices.Length - 1] = Vector3.up * -radius;
42         #endregion
43
44         #region Normals
45         Vector3[] normales = new Vector3[vertices.Length];
46         for (int n = 0; n < vertices.Length; n++)
47             normales[n] = vertices[n].normalized;
48         #endregion
49
```

```
50        #region UVs
51        Vector2[] uvs = new Vector2[vertices.Length];
52        uvs[0] = Vector2.up;
53        uvs[uvs.Length - 1] = Vector2.zero;
54        for (int lat = 0; lat < nbLat; lat++)
55            for (int lon = 0; lon <= nbLong; lon++)
56                uvs[lon + lat * (nbLong + 1) + 1] = new
                 Vector2((float)lon / nbLong, 1f - (float)(lat +
                 1) / (nbLat + 1));
57        #endregion
58
59        #region Triangles
60        int nbFaces = vertices.Length;
61        int nbTriangles = nbFaces * 2;
62        int nbIndexes = nbTriangles * 3;
63        int[] triangles = new int[nbIndexes];
64
65        //Top Cap
66        int i = 0;
67        for (int lon = 0; lon < nbLong; lon++)
68        {
69            triangles[i++] = lon + 2;
70            triangles[i++] = lon + 1;
71            triangles[i++] = 0;
72        }
73
74        //Middle
75        for (int lat = 0; lat < nbLat - 1; lat++)
76        {
77            for (int lon = 0; lon < nbLong; lon++)
78            {
79                int current = lon + lat * (nbLong + 1) + 1;
80                int next = current + nbLong + 1;
81
82                triangles[i++] = current;
83                triangles[i++] = current + 1;
84                triangles[i++] = next + 1;
85
86                triangles[i++] = current;
87                triangles[i++] = next + 1;
88                triangles[i++] = next;
89            }
90        }
91
```

```
92          //Bottom Cap
93          for (int lon = 0; lon < nbLong; lon++)
94          {
95              triangles[i++] = vertices.Length - 1;
96              triangles[i++] = vertices.Length - (lon + 2) - 1;
97              triangles[i++] = vertices.Length - (lon + 1) - 1;
98          }
99          #endregion
100
101         mesh.vertices = vertices;
102         mesh.normals = normales;
103         mesh.uv = uvs;
104         mesh.triangles = triangles;
105
106         mesh.RecalculateBounds();
107         mesh.Optimize();
108     }
109 }
```

As you can see, there is a lot that goes into generating a seemingly simple sphere. Luckily, we didn't have to write this algorithm from scratch. Primitive shapes are pretty well defined and can usually be found documented somewhere else. For more complex meshes, though, you will need to engineer them yourself.

In the beginning of *Code Snip 9.2*, we set Mesh and Mesh Filter. The Mesh object is what gets rendered, but we use Mesh Filter for general mesh manipulation. In the Start function, we make a call to our GenerateSphere function passing in a radius and latitude and longitude lines:

- Lines 15-18: In the GenerateSphere function, we add the MeshFilter component and clear the new MeshFilter to make sure it is ready to go.

- Lines 20-42: This script is broken up into regions so that it is a little more readable. In the Vertices region, we plot the points that we will then create triangles out of. The algorithm creates an array of Vector3 positions that represent the vertices. The vertices are calculated on a curved grid using the longitude and latitude lines. The curvature is calculated using sine and cosine, which are trigonometric functions for calculating angles.

- Lines 44-48: In the Normals region, we calculate the normal of each vertex. There is a Unity built-in function for this, called normalized. The normal of a vertex is the direction the vertex is facing.

- Lines `50-57`: The `UVs` region sets the mapping for texture wrapping. Textures use a set of coordinates to wrap the texture around a 3D object.

- Lines `59-99`: The `Triangles` region creates the list of triangles that the object will render. The triangles will be the face of our object. Each triangle is rendered with the given material using its set of three vertex positions. This algorithm creates a triangle in three parts: top, middle, and bottom.

- Lines `101-104`: At the end of the calculations, we assign the pieces from `Mesh Filter` to `Mesh`.

- Lines `106-107`: Lastly, we call two `Mesh` methods to finish our generated sphere. `RecalculateBounds` will make sure the volume of the new mesh is correctly calculated and optimize will attempt to make the object render faster to the screen. You'll need to add a `Mesh Renderer` and a component to the `Material` on the object. Also, be sure the object is in view of the camera if you don't see anything appear. You can also inspect the sphere in the **Scene** view while in the play mode. Now, if you create an empty GameObject, add this script and play the scene. You should see a sphere:

Procedurally generated sphere

# Adding randomization

Now we are going to add the same randomization to this sphere as we did the Unity primitive sphere. We just need to add our Randomize function at the end of the ProceduralSphere.cs script. *Code Snip 9.3* shows what that looks like:

```
1    private void GenerateSphere (float radius, int nbLong, int
     nbLat) {
2
...
3
4        mesh.vertices = vertices;
5        mesh.normals = normales;
6        mesh.uv = uvs;
7        mesh.triangles = triangles;
8
9        mesh.RecalculateBounds ();
10       mesh.Optimize ();
11
12       mesh.vertices = Randomize (vertices);
13   }
14
15   private Vector3 [] Randomize (Vector3 [] verts) {
16       Dictionary<Vector3, List<int>> dictionary = new
         Dictionary<Vector3, List<int>>();
17
18       for (int x = 0; x < verts.Length; x++) {
19
20           if (!dictionary.ContainsKey (verts [x])) {
21               dictionary.Add (verts [x], new List<int>());
22           }
23           dictionary [verts [x]] .Add (x);
24       }
25
26       foreach (KeyValuePair<Vector3, List<int>> pair in
         dictionary) {
27           Vector3 newPos = pair.Key * Random.Range (0.9f,
             1.1f);
28           foreach (int i in pair.Value) {
29
30               verts [i] = newPos;
31           }
32       }
33
34       return verts;
35   }
```

The update to the `ProceduralSphere` script simply adds the `Randomize` function to the end of the file and calls it at the end of the `GenerateSphere` function. This will have a very similar effect on its looks as the Unity primitive sphere. However, since we are procedurally generating the sphere, we are always one bad function call away from straining our system.

# Bad time and space complexities

Imagine if we needed to perform a task on each vertex after we moved only one. This would cause us to loop over the whole set of vertices multiple times. This would be more costly in time than even just generating a more complex sphere. The performance of our game is ultimately hurt with scripts like this.

As a demonstration of a bad time complexity, we will update our code slightly to simulate having to perform extra tasks on each vertex move.

 Save your scene and project before running this script, as it might crash Unity!

*Code Snip 9.4* shows the update for the demo:

```
1    void Start () {
2        GenerateSphere(1f, 10, 10);
3    }
4

...

5
6    private Vector3[] Randomize(Vector3[] verts) {
7        Dictionary<Vector3, List<int>> dictionary = new
         Dictionary<Vector3, List<int>>();
8
9        for (int x = 0; x < verts.Length; x++) {
10
11            if (!dictionary.ContainsKey(verts[x])) {
12                dictionary.Add(verts[x], new List<int>());
13            }
14            dictionary[verts[x]].Add(x);
15        }
16
17        foreach (KeyValuePair<Vector3, List<int>> pair in
         dictionary) {
18            Vector3 newPos = pair.Key * Random.Range(0.9f,
             1.1f);
```

```
19              foreach (int i in pair.Value) {
20
21                  verts[i] = newPos;
22                  for (int j = 0; j < mesh.vertexCount; j++) {
23                      Debug.Log("loading...");
24                  }
25              }
26          }
27
28      return verts;
29  }
```

We are going to lessen the number of longitude and latitude sections in the sphere as this script is very heavy in processing. Then, we will add lines 22-24. This is a loop through the set of vertices that make up the sphere. We make a Debug.Log call as some work to perform.

If you run this, you should notice your computer take 30 seconds to 1 minute processing before rendering the sphere to your screen. If you don't notice any time delay, then you have a very good computer. You can increase the longitude and latitude lines but do this in increments of 1.

The Debug.Log call actually takes quite a bit of time to complete as there is more work involved than you might think. This example is thus an exaggeration but should still be considered. We have exponentially increased the amount of time it will take to render the sphere because of our extra loop. Be aware of this time complexity moving forward.

This sort of thing can happen with *space* as well. When we say *space*, we mean the memory your computer can store at a time. To see an example of bad space complexity, we simply need to increase the sphere complexity to an unmanageable level.

Start by removing the loop from *Code Snip 9.4* on lines 22-24. Then, increase the longitude and latitude arguments in the GenerateSphere call on line 2 to over 300. If you run this updated code, you will get an error saying you have exceeded the maximum number of vertices.

These are good things to be aware of when working with 3D. As you can see, you can easily add some code that will either slow your system tremendously or break it outright. Good programmers always consider time and space complexities to keep performance as high as possible.

# Multi mesh planet

Now that we are able to generate a sphere and understand some of the pitfalls of 3D rendering, we are ready to generate our planet. Normally, the approach for generating a planet would be to generate a sphere and then generate a random texture called a height map. This is well covered and documented in free online resources. This would require quite a bit of work and extra plugins so it will be left to you to research on your own. We will take another approach that can be scripted easily.

We will generate multiple spheres and perform some manipulations on their geometry to give them each a unique character. We are also going to use a different type of sphere for this task. This sphere will be generated from a polygon called an Icosahedron. The algorithm for this primitive can be found at the Unity Wiki page, `http://wiki.unity3d.com/index.php/ProceduralPrimitives`.

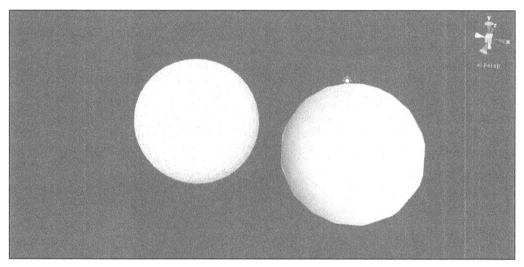

Icosahedron sphere on the left and polar sphere on the right

The **icosahedron sphere** is seamlessly created, meaning that there are fewer vertices and we can get rid of the vertex grouping functionality. This helps improve performance overall. We can do this with the polar sphere but the icosphere has a more uniform shape that will work better for the following example. The code to generate the icosahedron sphere is found at the same Unity Wiki page as the polar sphere.

We are going to write a single script that we can use and manipulate properties to create the terrain, water, and sky of our generated planet. Before we begin writing the script, we need to create some materials so that we can tell our spheres apart. Create a `Materials` folder in your `Assets` folder.

In the `Materials` folder, create a new `Material`. You can name this material `Land`. Then, you can follow the given steps:

1. Set **Shader** to **Standard**.
2. Set **Rendering Mode** to **Opaque**.
3. Set **Smoothness** to 0.

This will give us a nice flat land material. Next, we can make the water. Create a new material with the color blue and these properties:

1. Set **Shader** to **Standard**.
2. Set **Rendering Mode** to **Transparent**.
3. Set **Smoothness** to 0.7.

Lastly, we will make a sky material with a light blue color and the following properties:

1. Set **Shader** to **Standard**.
2. Set **Rendering Mode** to **Transparent**.
3. Set **Smoothness** to 0.2.

Now, in the editor, create four new empty GameObjects and call them `Land1`, `Land2`, `Water`, and `Sky` respectively. Make sure that they share the exact same XYZ position. Add a **Mesh Renderer** component to each object. Add a **Mesh Collider** component to `Land1` and `Land2`. And add the materials to the appropriate GameObjects.

Now we are ready to write the new script. Create a new script called `ProceduralPlanet.cs`. Then, open up the script for editing. *Code Snip 9.5* shows the new script in its entirety:

```
1 using UnityEngine;
2 using System.Collections;
3 using System.Collections.Generic;
4 using Random = UnityEngine.Random;
5
6 public class ProceduralPlanet : MonoBehaviour {
7
8      private struct TriangleIndices {
9           public int v1;
10          public int v2;
11          public int v3;
12
13          public TriangleIndices(int v1, int v2, int v3) {
```

```
14              this.v1 = v1;
15              this.v2 = v2;
16              this.v3 = v3;
17          }
18      }
19
20      private Mesh mesh;
21
22      public bool randomize;
23      public bool offset;
24      public bool invert;
25      public float rad;
26      public int detail;
27      public MeshCollider meshCollider;
28
29      // Use this for initialization
30      void Start () {
31          Create(rad, detail);
32
33          if (offset) {
34              Offset();
35          }
36
37          if (meshCollider) {
38              meshCollider.sharedMesh = mesh;
39          }
40
41  }
42
43  private void Offset () {
44          int offset = Random.Range(1, 7);
45
46          int offsetMod = Random.Range(0, 2);
47          if (offsetMod == 0) {
48              offsetMod = -1;
49          }
50
51          Vector3 offsetVec = new Vector3();
52          switch (offset) {
53              case 1:
54                  offsetVec = new Vector3(Random.Range(0.01f,
                    0.05f), 0, 0) * offsetMod;
55                  break;
56              case 2:
```

```
57              offsetVec = new Vector3(0, Random.Range(0.01f,
                0.05f), 0) * offsetMod;
58              break;
59          case 3:
60              offsetVec = new Vector3(0, 0,
                Random.Range(0.01f, 0.05f)) * offsetMod;
61              break;
62      }
63      transform.position = transform.position += offsetVec;
64  }
65
66  // return index of point in the middle of p1 and p2
67  private int getMiddlePoint(int p1, int p2, ref List<Vector3>
    vertices, ref Dictionary<long, int> cache, float radius) {
68      // first check if we have it already
69      bool firstIsSmaller = p1 < p2;
70      long smallerIndex = firstIsSmaller ? p1 : p2;
71      long greaterIndex = firstIsSmaller ? p2 : p1;
72      long key = (smallerIndex << 32) + greaterIndex;
73
74      int ret;
75      if (cache.TryGetValue(key, out ret)) {
76          return ret;
77      }
78
79      // not in cache, calculate it
80      Vector3 point1 = vertices[p1];
81      Vector3 point2 = vertices[p2];
82      Vector3 middle = new Vector3
83      (
84          (point1.x + point2.x) / 2f,
85          (point1.y + point2.y) / 2f,
86          (point1.z + point2.z) / 2f
87      );
88
89      // add vertex makes sure point is on unit sphere
90      int i = vertices.Count;
91      vertices.Add(middle.normalized * radius);
92
93      // store it, return index
94      cache.Add(key, i);
95
96      return i;
97  }
```

```
98
99      public void Create(float radius, int recursionLevel) {
100         MeshFilter filter =
            gameObject.AddComponent<MeshFilter>();
101         mesh = filter.mesh;
102         mesh.Clear();
103
104         List<Vector3> vertList = new List<Vector3>();
105         Dictionary<long, int> middlePointIndexCache = new
            Dictionary<long, int>();
106
107         // create 12 vertices of a icosahedron
108         float t = (1f + Mathf.Sqrt(5f)) / 2f;
109
110         vertList.Add(new Vector3(-1f, t, 0f).normalized *
            radius);
111         vertList.Add(new Vector3(1f, t, 0f).normalized *
            radius);
112         vertList.Add(new Vector3(-1f, -t, 0f).normalized *
            radius);
113         vertList.Add(new Vector3(1f, -t, 0f).normalized *
            radius);
114
115         vertList.Add(new Vector3(0f, -1f, t).normalized *
            radius);
116         vertList.Add(new Vector3(0f, 1f, t).normalized *
            radius);
117         vertList.Add(new Vector3(0f, -1f, -t).normalized *
            radius);
118         vertList.Add(new Vector3(0f, 1f, -t).normalized *
            radius);
119
120         vertList.Add(new Vector3(t, 0f, -1f).normalized *
            radius);
121         vertList.Add(new Vector3(t, 0f, 1f).normalized *
            radius);
122         vertList.Add(new Vector3(-t, 0f, -1f).normalized *
            radius);
123         vertList.Add(new Vector3(-t, 0f, 1f).normalized *
            radius);
124
125
126         // create 20 triangles of the icosahedron
127         List<TriangleIndices> faces = new
            List<TriangleIndices>();
```

```
128
129          // 5 faces around point 0
130          faces.Add(new TriangleIndices(0, 11, 5));
131          faces.Add(new TriangleIndices(0, 5, 1));
132          faces.Add(new TriangleIndices(0, 1, 7));
133          faces.Add(new TriangleIndices(0, 7, 10));
134          faces.Add(new TriangleIndices(0, 10, 11));
135
136          // 5 adjacent faces
137          faces.Add(new TriangleIndices(1, 5, 9));
138          faces.Add(new TriangleIndices(5, 11, 4));
139          faces.Add(new TriangleIndices(11, 10, 2));
140          faces.Add(new TriangleIndices(10, 7, 6));
141          faces.Add(new TriangleIndices(7, 1, 8));
142
143          // 5 faces around point 3
144          faces.Add(new TriangleIndices(3, 9, 4));
145          faces.Add(new TriangleIndices(3, 4, 2));
146          faces.Add(new TriangleIndices(3, 2, 6));
147          faces.Add(new TriangleIndices(3, 6, 8));
148          faces.Add(new TriangleIndices(3, 8, 9));
149
150          // 5 adjacent faces
151          faces.Add(new TriangleIndices(4, 9, 5));
152          faces.Add(new TriangleIndices(2, 4, 11));
153          faces.Add(new TriangleIndices(6, 2, 10));
154          faces.Add(new TriangleIndices(8, 6, 7));
155          faces.Add(new TriangleIndices(9, 8, 1));
156
157
158          // refine triangles
159          for (int i = 0; i < recursionLevel; i++) {
160              List<TriangleIndices> faces2 = new
                 List<TriangleIndices>();
161              foreach (var tri in faces) {
162                  // replace triangle by 4 triangles
163                  int a = getMiddlePoint(tri.v1, tri.v2, ref
                     vertList, ref middlePointIndexCache, radius);
164                  int b = getMiddlePoint(tri.v2, tri.v3, ref
                     vertList, ref middlePointIndexCache, radius);
165                  int c = getMiddlePoint(tri.v3, tri.v1, ref
                     vertList, ref middlePointIndexCache, radius);
166
167                  faces2.Add(new TriangleIndices(tri.v1, a, c));
```

```
168                    faces2.Add(new TriangleIndices(tri.v2, b, a));
169                    faces2.Add(new TriangleIndices(tri.v3, c, b));
170                    faces2.Add(new TriangleIndices(a, b, c));
171                }
172                faces = faces2;
173            }
174
175            mesh.vertices = vertList.ToArray();
176
177            List<int> triList = new List<int>();
178            for (int i = 0; i < faces.Count; i++) {
179                triList.Add(faces[i].v1);
180                triList.Add(faces[i].v2);
181                triList.Add(faces[i].v3);
182            }
183
184            mesh.triangles = triList.ToArray();
185            mesh.uv = new Vector2[mesh.vertices.Length];
186
187            Vector3[] normales = new Vector3[vertList.Count];
188            for (int i = 0; i < normales.Length; i++)
189                normales[i] = vertList[i].normalized;
190
191
192            mesh.normals = normales;
193
194            if (invert) {
195                // Reverse the triangles
196                int[] triangles = mesh.triangles;
197                for (int i = 0; i < triangles.Length; i += 3) {
198                    int j = triangles[i];
199                    triangles[i] = triangles[i + 2];
200                    triangles[i + 2] = j;
201                }
202                mesh.triangles = triangles;
203
204                // Reverse the normals;
205                Vector3[] normals = mesh.normals;
206                for (int i = 0; i < normals.Length; i++)
207                    normals[i] = -normals[i];
208                mesh.normals = normals;
209            }
210
```

```
211            mesh.RecalculateBounds();
212            mesh.Optimize();
213
214        if (randomize)
215            mesh.vertices = Randomize(mesh.vertices);
216    }
217
218    Vector3[] Randomize(Vector3[] verts) {
219
220        for (int x = 0; x < verts.Length; x++) {
221            Vector3 newPos = verts[x] * Random.Range(0.95f,
                1.03f);
222            verts[x] = newPos;
223        }
224
225            return verts;
226    }
227 }
```

Most of this script is the algorithm for generating the icosahedron sphere. Then, at the end is our `Randomize` function but without the vertex grouping functionality. Despite the size of the script, it only requires a brief explanation of its components. It is left to you to research and understand the mathematics behind geometrically constructing an icosahedron. Let's take a quick look at *Code snip 9.5*:

- `Lines 8-18`: The struct `TriangleIndices` is used as a helper class to store information on the triangles of the icosahedron.

- `Lines 20-27`: Here, we set a reference to the Mesh and set some public variables that will be used to determine the properties of the spheres:

    - `bool randomize` will be set if we wish to randomize the location of the vertices to create a terrain.

    - `bool offset` will be set if we want to offset the sphere slightly so that they aren't perfectly aligned. We will do this with the land to make one or more sides of the planet terrain heavy.

    - `bool invert` will invert the triangles so the material is drawn on the inside of the sphere. This will be used for the sky.

    - `float rad` is the radius of the sphere.

    - `int detail` is how many triangles we want to generate in the sphere. This is a multiplier, not a value.

    - `MeshCollider meshCollider` will determine if characters can walk on the mesh or not.

- Lines 43-64: The Offset function will run if offset is set to true. This function will randomly choose a number that corresponds to a direction in which the sphere will be offset, either -X, X, -Y, Y, -Z, or Z. Then, the sphere is offset in that direction by a small random amount. This will make the land appear through the water more on one side than the other.

- Lines 67-97: GetMiddlePoint is a helper function to the Create function. It is used as an interpolation method. This function will return the point at which an edge can be split into two separate edges.

- Lines 99-216: The Create method runs the icosahedron generation and interpolation into a sphere.

- Lines 218-226: Last is our Randomize function without the vertex grouping, which is a much faster solution given the appropriate amount of memory

Now, we can add this script to each of our empty GameObjects, Land1, Land2, Water, and Sky. Each one will have a different use of the public properties. So, after you add the script to each object, set these property values.

For Land1 and Land2, set the following values:

- Check **Randomize**
- Check **Offset**
- Set **Rad** to 5
- Set **Detail** to 2
- Add the Mesh Collider component to the Mesh Collider field

For Water, set the following:

- Set **Rad** to 4.92
- Set **Detail** to 5

For Sky, set the following:

- Check **Invert**
- Set **Rad** to 6.5
- Set **Detail** to 5

Make sure that the empty objects are in view of the camera and give it a play. You should see your very own procedurally generated planet. You can experiment with the properties or add more objects to see what happens.

Procedurally generated planet

# Exploring the planet

Now that we have generated a planet, it would be awesome if we could explore the surface of it. As a fun bonus, we will add a first-person-view controller, so we can explore our planets. Fortunately for us, someone has already tackled the problem of spherical gravity in Unity, so all we will have to do is plug and play.

You can get the script for this section either from the example files or from its source at `https://github.com/SebLague/Spherical-Gravity` by SebLague. There is also a video at that location where you can see how the scripts work. The scripts that are included are the `FirstPersonController.cs`, `GravityAttractor.cs`, and `GravityBody.cs`.

You are welcome to view the video to get an explanation on the code in these scripts. We are just going to plug them in and use them as they are, though. You'll want to add the `GravityAttractor` script to the `Water` object. Set a tag for the `Water` sphere to `Planet`. Then, create a capsule for our first person controller by navigating to **GameObject | 3D Object | Capsule** from the top menu and naming it `Player`.

Place the main camera as a child of the `Player` object. You'll want to have the camera project from the upper portion of the capsule, where eyes might be. For this example, scaling the player to 0.055 worked well. Also, set the main camera's **Field of View** to `32` and the **Clipping Planes to Near**: `0.01` and **Far**: `7.54`. This should work well for the size of the sphere we are using.

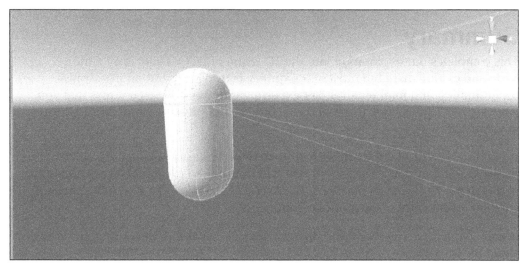

The first-person camera placement

Add the **GravityBody** and **FirstPersonController** to the player. For the **FirstPersonController**, setting the **Mouse Sensitivity X & Y** to `1` and the **Walk Speed** to `0.5` worked well. Be sure to place the player outside the generated radius of the planet; otherwise, it won't read the collider meshes correctly. Then, play the scene and explore your planet.

The first-person view of the planet

You'll be able to see through the sky as it is transparent. You can also slightly see through the water areas. There is no collider on the water mesh so you can walk through those areas. In some cases, you will go under the water mesh, and since the material doesn't render on the back side of the mesh, it will appear as though it isn't there.

# Summary

This completes our exploration into the 3D realm of PCG. There is a lot more to do and explore here but most of it requires a strong foundation in graphics programming and mathematics. Try experimenting with the techniques that you have learned in this book to generate 3D objects and possibly randomizing them in some way.

A good start to your self-learning would be to procedurally change the colors of your planet. See if you can write a script that will randomize the colors on the materials of the planet as we did in *Chapter 5, Randomized Items*. You can also refine the land creation process and make modular continents as well.

In this chapter, we discussed the changes from 2D versus 3D rendering. You learned about the importance of space and time complexity. You learned that there is usually more than one way to make a 3D object. Lastly, you learned that PCG with 3D requires quite a bit of highly specific mathematics.

You learned all about PCG both in 2D and 3D. We have completed all of the programming that this book has to offer. The next chapter isn't so much about coding PCG as it is discussing the future of PCG and where it plans to take us.

# 10
# Generating the Future

Throughout the book you've learned a lot about the concept of PCG and its different forms. You have also had the chance to experience PCG, first hand, by designing and implementing PCG algorithms. You built the core game play of a 2D *Roguelike* game that can generate content forever. You also implemented a 3D planet generator that not only looked good from afar, but we were also able to explore it in first person.

PCG doesn't end there though. There are still a lot of topics that we didn't cover such as generating textures and story lines or allowing the player to generate content. There is a lot that can be done and has yet to be done in the world of PCG for games.

In this chapter, we will go over the main categories of game content and discuss how these, sometimes very different, areas can be procedurally generated. This chapter will give you a basic idea of how to approach your further PCG learning. It's likely that following is a category of content that you didn't even think about procedurally generating. And, hopefully, this chapter will help inspire you to try new PCG techniques in game development.

Here are the categories that we will cover in this chapter:

- Models
- Items
- Levels
- Textures
- Terrain
- Physics
- Animations
- AI
- Story
- Player sandbox

PCG has been around since the beginning of game development. This is because video games were created by programmers. Everything had to be procedurally generated in the very beginning. In the early days of computing, the same modern resources were not available. Early computers lacked the memory to store game models for characters and levels, and performance was too limited to display complex graphics. PCG has been around since the beginning, but it has a brighter future now than ever before due to our advances in technology.

# Models

3D models, as you saw in *Chapter 9*, *Generating a 3D Planet*, can be extraordinarily complicated. It is natural we created programs that allow designers to sculpt in a digital 3D space as opposed to trying to create an algorithm that would generate these 3D models. A simple sphere can take thousands of lines of code to create alone.

Allowing a person to sculpt and see the creation of the model as it is being created allows for an unparalleled level of detail. It would simply take too long to try and procedurally generate every 3D model in a game. So, we generally stick to procedurally manipulating models.

The trade-off then is to make small pieces of a model that can be widely used and then having those procedurally constructed into a whole model at runtime. The effect is that we create a game world that is unique to that playthrough. It could be possible that the game world morphs every time the player starts a new game or just that this game world is unique to another player's game world.

Left: simple model made from modules; Right: more complex model with same modules

The method of modularizing game models has its pros and cons. Designers will design smaller pieces but might have to do just as much work, if not more, to create enough modules to fill a game. The developer also has the extra task of placing these modules correctly in the game so that they make sense to the player. The outcome of this is that we can have unique environments for each player and we don't have to program the exact geometry of every single model. If we generate a level layout, we can then swap in the model modules at random fairly easily.

We can also apply the method of modularization to all of our 3D models including items and characters. Character generation is even simpler as most characters in a game will have a similar form. If you put the character together with modules, then you can swap them out as well. If we choose, we can take this to smaller layers of detail.

Character building modules with modules

The final piece here is that modules can have parameters of differentiation to easily make small adjustments and increase uniqueness. These parameters can be anything from color to minor model module additions to the current module or vertex movements. These parameters can further the differentiation in models and drastically increase the number of unique models in a game.

Two characters with the same modules but different parameters

Modulating models in video games opens the doors to generating unique models in every game playthrough if we wanted. We can apply it to levels, items, characters, or any 3D modeled construct. But the power is really in finding new ways to make smaller modules so that the modules compound to make seemingly infinite possibilities. This method has the drawback of needing a lot of processing power and it might use more memory when it fully expands as compared to traditional methods.

You can pursue areas of further learning such as the field of graphics programming to gain more knowledge on PCG with 3D models. You will need a strong understanding of 3D space mathematics, which it includes but is not limited to calculus, linear algebra, and geometry. The study of computer science can usually include most of what you need to know.

# Items

Besides using parameters, another way that model generation compounds is through item generation. If a character is built of armor pieces and uses weapons that are procedurally generated, then each one of those pieces has properties that can be manipulated or modularized. Just like our sword from *Chapter 6, Generating Modular Weapons*, the item will be made of a certain amount of pieces. However, imagine if each of the pieces was then made of another set of pieces and so on.

Compounding model generation through item generation can create a truly unique experience. However, having to generate that many objects would be costly to our performance due to the amount of time and space it would require. It would also be hard on the player if every single object in the game looked different. People look for patterns.

One option would be to generate an item and then store a reference to that model for later use. By reusing some things, we give the player some patterns to work with. An example of this would be to generate all swords that do fire damage to be rendered with a red glow.

We still need to consider things like overloading our system, machine, or even the player. We need to strike a balance when it comes to model generation. You can potentially create a system that can generate trillions of unique objects, but without the proper processing power and memory management, it might not be a practical solution. It could be too overwhelming for the player to have that many options.

Item generation is another form of model generation or sprite generation. For further study, you will need a foundation in 2D and 3D space mathematics. However, items usually impact how the player interacts with their environment. So in addition to programming and mathematics, it would be beneficial to spend some time studying game design and user experience. Being able to fully conceptualize the balance that needs to be applied to item generation makes you a well-rounded developer.

# Levels

Props used to fill the empty space in levels are similar, in this sense of creating patterns. We can create patterns with our props to lead the player to places of interest. An example of this would be to generate the interior of a building with items we might expect to see in that building. We need to think like a level designer in this sense.

An old time tavern or bar prop set

The challenge would be to place the props in such a way that is believable. One way would be to tag the prop with a general descriptor such as a table or a chair. Then, tag an area in a modular room where a table might show up with the table tag. Any table variant prop will now only generate on table areas.

Levels push the boundaries of PCG simply because they can be as small as a room of a house or as big as a planet. We can be very minute with our modulation if we choose. Either we can create an environment by connecting modules, or we can simply set up a space and allow modules to populate the area.

Currently, technology has reached a point, giving us, as game developers, a choice to make. We can make contained levels within a linear or semi expansive game or we can make a universe full of procedurally generated levels. Either choice has pros and cons. Besides the requirement difference in processing power and memory, there is a question of game design. I need to be certain that the experience we wish to deliver to the player requires PCG or we will be wasting development time and resources.

Modular dungeon versus a procedurally generated world (left: Daggerfall, right: No Man's Sky)

# Texture

One thing that really ties together a level or character design is texture. This is the very reason textures are designed by human hands. They usually convey a specific tone. But one thing that we can use to our advantage is the fact that a lot of textures happen naturally.

This would be similar to the stripes on a tiger. Realistically, we wouldn't see a constant pattern around the tiger, though. We would have to break the tiger up into sections of texture such as, the most prominent stripes would be on the back and they would fade as it wrapped to the stomach.

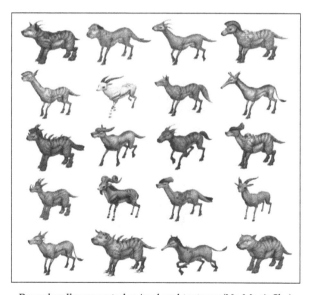

Procedurally generated animal and textures (No Man's Sky)

One way to accomplish this is to have animals of a similar shape so that the texture map will apply similarly to the different animal models. The textures can be tinted in different colors so that the animal shape and color will stand out over the texture, which is more ambient. Also, making the colors of the texture similar will blend the texture patterns and make the texture more subtle and less noticeable.

In theory, textures should be easy to generate. We can reference naturally occurring patterns such as fractals to create random yet organic looking textures. However, in practice, texture generation requires a bit more thought than just applying random patterns. This brings us back to the ideas of game design and user experience.

The player is looking for patterns similar to the ones they see in reality. If you have a game full of random textures, it can be disorienting for the player. Instead, we try to find ways to replicate familiar patterns such as stones on a building, the bark of a tree, or stripes on an animal. This leads us to, again, a modularization solution such as the one described previously.

# Terrain

Texture and terrain can have similar procedural generation beginnings. With either, we can use a fractal or noise patterns as a basis. We can create a height map that can be wrapped around objects. An alternative for our planet in *Chapter 9, Generating a 3D Planet*, would have been to use a Perlin noise distortion height map.

A height map is a texture that has 3D qualities. You would then apply the height map texture to the 3D model to give the model a 3D texture. As you can see in the following figure, this is an easy way to create a terrain.

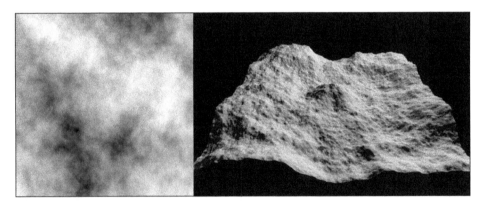

Noise image used to create height map

Besides the actual texture of the ground, tons of work has gone into making tree and foliage generators. Terrain is one of the better defined constructs in PCG. This is a good starting point for anyone learning 3D PCG.

# Physics

Physics is very well defined as a theory, so it translates well to programming simulations and subsequently, game design. However, physics is a separate field from PCG. Still, physics can be used to aid us in our execution of PCG.

An example of using physics as a mechanism of PCG is the popular mobile game, *Angry Birds*. In *Angry Birds*, a modular structure is presented but it then has physics applied to it as a means to restructure it. The effects of the physics create new structures that then impact how the game is played.

The Angry Birds' gameplay is based on physics

The trade-off is that physics requires a lot of processing power. Current technology now provides dedicated hardware to processing just the physical simulations in games. It can add very unique game playthrough.

Physics is its own field of study, so it is a good place to start when researching new ways to apply physics to PCG. There are a lot of physics engines available such as the Open Dynamic Engine, so it might be more beneficial to research new ways to apply current physics systems to PCG. An idea would be to add destructible structures to your game that then leave ruins when they are destroyed.

# Animation

Animation generation is more common than one might think. Have you ever played a game where an NPC turned to look in your direction? This is a procedurally generated animation.

Mr. I in Mario 64, changing the direction it looks in toward Mario

These types of animations are more intuitively created procedurally. A similar example is an NPC moving towards you as you fled. The NPC would have to procedurally generate the path and animate its position through it. This is only a partial animation, though, as we would still have to animate the walk or run animation as well. The walk/run animation would be much harder to generate procedurally so we usually use key frame animation here.

Animation is something that has been studied in the academic realm for a while. Animating physical reactions is a big part of this study, but natural movement comes up a lot too. We use key frame animation for things like movement because we need the animations to look believable or it breaks immersion. However, it might be the case that procedurally generated animations are preferred eventually.

An example of procedurally generating an animation that relied on believability might be if you were to take a randomly generated creature that we knew would walk on some number of feet, we generated the movement animation. We would place an alternating back and forth motion on the feet and an alternating swing or sway on the body. Perhaps even add alternating animations on any other limbs as well.

Animation is another field that can be studied all on its own. If you were looking for ways to generate animation with PCG, it would be worth your time to study key frame animation. Usually, when generating animations, there is a certain amount of physics involved as well. If you imagine walking, it is a very physics-intensive action where your body is constantly fighting against gravity.

# AI

Artificial intelligence, like physics and animation, is also its own field of study. We can use PCG to enhance certain aspects of AI. In *Chapter 7, Adaptive Difficulty,* we used PCG to rewrite a section of our AI. This isn't always the most practical approach though.

AI for games can be easily visualized as a state machine or a graph of connected behaviors. Some actions in the AI graph might lead to others or some situations might cause an AI to enact a certain behavior. In the following diagram, we see rectangles represented as states and arrows representing states transitioning into other states. This network of states can be as complex or simple as we like.

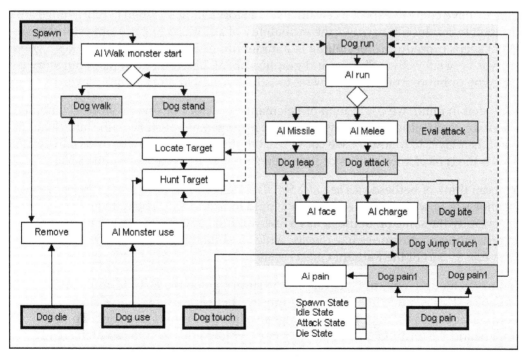

AI state machine

An example of a complex AI state machine is Bethesda's Radiant AI. This AI system has the NPCs react to the actions of the player, but also has them generate a daily routine. They can go to work, travel, and some might set out to attempt assassinations. These behaviors are programmed separately, but then the routine is generated at runtime.

Thinking of AI behaviors as content that can be manipulated allows us to use the principles of PCG to generate and manipulate our AI in-game. However, there are many more ways to implement artificial intelligence other than using a state machine. With that in mind, it would be a good start to study artificial intelligence in general to find the best ways to apply PCG to it.

# Story

Adding in the functionality for a player to influence the outcome of a game story can look much like a state machine as well. Usually, these state machines are much less complicated though. There are certain things that can't be generated well quite yet like voiceovers in terms of tone and conveying emotion.

Players have come to expect a certain level of storytelling so when certain things are difficult to produce, it narrows the availability of additions like multiple storylines. What keeps procedural storytelling to a minimum is the fact that what makes a good story is very subjective. Physics and graphics are all based on hard math but story is based on opinion. And we don't want to deliver a subpar story to our player.

With that in mind, we could map out elements to a story or several stories combined. Then, we could either randomly choose the arrangement of story path states that we want the player to follow, or we could react to the player's behavior in certain events. This is the typical approach as of right now, but usually on a very subtle scale.

You can think of Bethesda's *The Elder Scrolls* series or BioWare's *Mass Effect* series as examples of how a player-driven story would look and feel. The outcome of the story is generally the same or, at most, has a few variants. In general, we see more success in generating micro-stories like quests, which is something we see in *The Elder Scrolls 5: Skyrim* as part of the Radiant Quests system.

In theory, though, you can generate whole stories given the right formula and variables. This is much like generating music. There is a structure to a story with certain areas that can be interchangeable like the sounds of a song. To fully understand the formula and extent of a story, you would need to research creative storytelling, just like you would research music theory to better generate music.

# The player sandbox

The player sandbox has become very popular lately. Even some games that have a linearly progressing story will provide open areas for the player to explore and generally progress the story at their own will. Allowing the player to do as they will is a form of content generation. It is also the other way to procedurally generate story.

Hello Games' *No Man's Sky* is a giant sandbox that is meant for the player to explore. There is no formal story, per say, but the player will go on many adventures simply exploring the game universe. This is one answer to procedurally generating story.

The sandbox is also a good way to generate content simply by constructing some tools and letting the player build their own world. Keep in mind that procedural generation does not always mean random generation. Allowing the player to build their own experience has the same effect, if not providing more immersion, then randomly generating the experience for them.

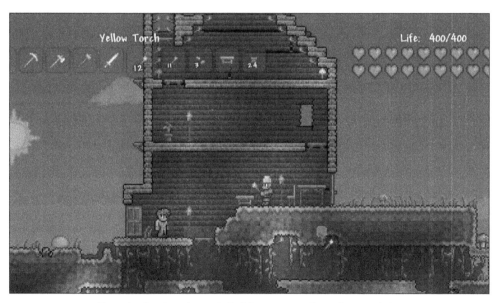

Terraria allowing players to build structures of any shape and size

# Summary

Even though randomization makes our procedures more spontaneous, it isn't always the correct path to take in PCG. You should be willing to explore the more involved route of fleshing out the modules or states to provide the player the best possible experience. In some cases, you should look to constrain your PCG to some parameters and tight bounds, while other times, you might want to turn over control to the payer entirely and let them choose their own fate.

In this chapter, we discussed the many ways we can apply PCG. However, the discussion of PCG goes far beyond this book and Unity. You did learn the different areas to begin your research of PCG in and the various fields in which it can be applied.

PCG is a great idea. We can generate whole universes at runtime, making our file size incredibly small while making our game incredibly huge. We can use it to spend less time designing art for our game by reusing art modules in inventive ways. We can make every playthrough of a game unique.

PCG is not a new concept, but as computers become more capable so does PCG. Fewer people can do more by making game development PCG heavy and using it wisely. PCG has a bright and uniquely random future ahead of it.

# Index

## Symbols

## A

## B

## C

## D

# W

Thank you for buying
**Procedural Content Generation for Unity Game Development**

## About Packt Publishing

Packt, pronounced 'packed', published its first book, *Mastering phpMyAdmin for Effective MySQL Management*, in April 2004, and subsequently continued to specialize in publishing highly focused books on specific technologies and solutions.

Our books and publications share the experiences of your fellow IT professionals in adapting and customizing today's systems, applications, and frameworks. Our solution-based books give you the knowledge and power to customize the software and technologies you're using to get the job done. Packt books are more specific and less general than the IT books you have seen in the past. Our unique business model allows us to bring you more focused information, giving you more of what you need to know, and less of what you don't.

Packt is a modern yet unique publishing company that focuses on producing quality, cutting-edge books for communities of developers, administrators, and newbies alike. For more information, please visit our website at www.packtpub.com.

## Writing for Packt

We welcome all inquiries from people who are interested in authoring. Book proposals should be sent to author@packtpub.com. If your book idea is still at an early stage and you would like to discuss it first before writing a formal book proposal, then please contact us; one of our commissioning editors will get in touch with you.

We're not just looking for published authors; if you have strong technical skills but no writing experience, our experienced editors can help you develop a writing career, or simply get some additional reward for your expertise.

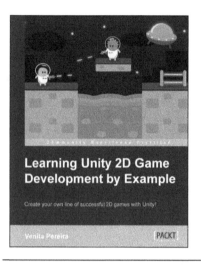

## Learning Unity 2D Game Development by Example

ISBN: 978-1-78355-904-6          Paperback: 266 pages

Create your own line of successful 2D games with Unity!

1. Dive into 2D game development with no previous experience.

2. Learn how to use the new Unity 2D toolset.

3. Create and deploy your very own 2D game with confidence.

## Unity 4.x Game Development by Example Beginner's Guide

ISBN: 978-1-84969-526-8          Paperback: 572 pages

A seat-of-your-pants manual for building fun, groovy little games quickly with Unity 4.x

1. Learn the basics of the Unity 3D game engine by building five small, functional game projects.

2. Explore simplification and iteration techniques that will make you more successful as a game developer.

3. Take Unity for a spin with a refreshingly humorous approach to technical manuals.

Please check **www.PacktPub.com** for information on our titles

PUBLISHING

**Getting Started with Unity 4 Scripting**

Juan Sebastian Muñoz

[PACKT]

## Getting Started with Unity 4 Scripting [Video]

ISBN: 978-1-84969-612-8      Duration: 02:06:54 hours

Harness the power of scripting in Unity 4 to build great games

1. A great resource for anyone new to Unity 4 scripting.

2. Clear step-by-step explanations for each line of code.

3. Create custom components that interact with Unity's game engine components.

4. Enhance your game with an easy-to-use and extendable input system that works on leading game platforms.

**Unity 3D Game Development by Example**

Adam Maxwell

[PACKT]

## Unity 3D Game Development by Example [Video]

ISBN: 978-1-84969-530-5      Duration: 02:30 hours

Learn how Unity3D "Thinks" by understanding Unity's UI and project structure to start building fun games in Unity 3D right away

1. 2 and a half hours of Unity screencast tutorials, broken into bite-sized sections.

2. Create 3D graphics, sound, and challenging gameplay.

3. Build game UI, high score tables, and other extra features.

4. Program powerful game logic with C# scripting.

Please check **www.PacktPub.com** for information on our titles

www.ingramcontent.com/pod-product-compliance
Lightning Source LLC
Chambersburg PA
CBHW060537060326
40690CB00017B/3521